VOCATIONAL CAPABILITIES OF SANGUINE PERSONALITIES AND BLENDS.

Discover Your Vocational Capabilities As A Sanguine.

Princewill Ejims

TABLE OF CONTENTS

DEDICATION:

First to Almighty God, the giver of all wisdom and inspiration to conceive and put thoughts together in writing this book. Secondly, to all predominant sanguine personalities who will find this book helpful in discovering their natural vocational strengths and capabilities in their job or career pursuit. And finally to everyone who appreciates the subject of temperament and its overwhelming influence on our personality.

ABOUT THE BOOK:

Vocational Capabilities Of Sanguine Personalities And Blends; is specifically written for predominant sanguine personalities. The objective of the book is to enable these air personalities and their blends to through the knowledge and understanding of inherited temperaments discover their natural vocational strengths, and the best jobs, careers or profession these strengths will enable them to be effortlessly and exceptionally successful in. Unless the job gives him the freedom and opportunity to socialize, and freely display his exuberance, a sanguine is arguably the least successful in routines that seems to cage him, or in any personal endeavor that is not people-centered, and will of course rarely allow him to freely express his emotions. For he usually believes that with people, he can always achieve his desires. Consequently in this book, you will discover;

. **Your innate vocational strengths as a sanguine,**

. **Best Jobs and Careers for your personality,**

. **Best Jobs and Careers for your personality blends,**

. **Most lucrative digital or tech jobs that suits your personality,**

. The major weakness you need to overcome in order to be more successful, and how you can.

ABOUT THE AUTHOR:

Princewill Ejims is a behavioral psychology expert with specialization in personality types and inherited temperaments which determines the traits, and influences the behavioral pattern of every human being in various aspects of life. His years of experience in this field has enabled him to write several blog posts and books about the behavioral patterns of the four temperament types, and how they influence what we do and how we do them. He has written and published books like;

-How to live with a choleric sweetheart.

-Melancholy personality vocational handbook,

-Temperament compatibility in marriage: A comprehensive guide to marital success.

-Demystifying The Melancholy Personality In Erotic Relationship: Understanding Your Melancholy Sweetheart, and

-How To Deal With A Sanguine Personality In A Relationship: Understand, Deal With Your Exuberant Sanguine Sweetheart.

He is the founder of Global Impact Outreach GIO. It's a non-profit organization saddled with the responsibility of helping people discover their temperament with its inherent strengths and weaknesses, so that they will be able to function effectively, and in sync with their personality and live to their full potentials without necessarily undermining themselves. The core areas of the organization are; marriage counseling, career guidance and development, leadership training, and personal development. He is married to Elizabeth Princewill Ejims, and together they have two daughters; Jewel and Adira.

You can reach him on;

+2348101362837

princewillejimsblog@gmail.com

Subscribe to my blog: https://princewillejimsblog.com

All scriptural quotations in this book were taken from the New King James version unless otherwise stated. All quotes in the text box are exclusively those of the author. Unauthorized usage through any means without the permission of the author is prohibited.

FOREWORD:

If you work in a big organization or establishment, and if you are observant enough you should of course be able to profile four categories of people and how they work or do their jobs. You have probably come across the first categories who are usually calm and collected, organized, thrives in routines, and always do their job with meticulous-patience, calmness, and efficiency as long as the job does not require venturing into uncharted and unfamiliar territories. The second categories rarely begin their job without adequate planning and conceptualizing strategies to enable them do a perfect job. These categories unlike the first, may not be scared of going into unfamiliar territories or embarking on a new task, but they are often skeptical about succeeding in those territories and easily expresses pessimism whenever a new task is presented, since they always too easily discover roadblocks or conjure up idealisms that they feel may become impediments towards adequately charting that territory. But regardless of their fears, they possess the innate capabilities to ultimately succeed. Now we come to the third category, these categories of people are workaholics who often drives you overboard with their work rate and high productivity. They enjoy field work a lot. Too much detail, analysis, and long range committee planning usually bores them; for they believe in going into the field and getting the job done asap. Obviously, they are not scared of going into uncharted territories or new and difficult task. And finally, you have probably worked with a colleague or come across someone who rarely stays in his office alone for too long. It is either his office is a beehive of activities where he frequently interface with people, or he may visit you ten times in your office for chitchats before break time or close of work for the day. These categories are very efficient in jobs that always expose them daily to people, and those that allows them to freely express their emotions. But any job that will subject them to being too meticulous, thorough, highly disciplined, and requires too much strategic thinking and planning is usually boring to him. And as for been assigned a new task that he is unfamiliar with, or getting into uncharted territory. He may initially and immediately bluster about his ability to get the job done, and he is usually the first to express his readiness. But when it is time to get in there and do the job, you will more often than not find him taking the back seat.

Basically, these are the four categories of people and how they usually do or approach their jobs. Some industry experts have made use of different social styles such as; amiable, analytical, driving, and expressive respectively to describe them. However, Hippocrates in his temperament theory of humorism called them; phlegmatic, melancholy, choleric, and sanguine respectively. But for the purpose of this book, we are specific, or focused on the latter which is the sanguine, to discover his natural vocational strengths and capabilities that will enable him to effortlessly succeed in certain jobs and careers that ranks even with these strengths and qualities. As a predominant sanguine and even as a non-sanguine personality. Perhaps you're an employer, this book will be of immense benefit to you. It will either help you to know the right jobs or careers for you as a sanguine where you will function effectively in, or help you as an employer to fix the right persons in the right positions where their natural strengths and capabilities will enable them to effortlessly do their jobs, and be efficient and productive.

INTRODUCTION.

There is usually something very desirable about every good job which could make us want to consider it or consistently engage in it. But the most desirable jobs are doubtlessly those that are in agreement with our natural vocational strengths and capabilities. These are the jobs or careers that of course enables us to either be more creative while doing them, be perfect and impeccable in our delivery, accomplish so much with minimal effort, and subsequently have a satisfactory feeling of fulfilment that we have done a great job. It's basically for this reason that while some people hate or despise their jobs because they struggle to do it, lack the motivation to be efficient in it, and therefore feels so unproductive and hopeless. Others are hitherto relishing their jobs and are continuously advancing in it. Our job or career is an important part of our life. For next to God, is our marriage and family, then career. It is of course the reason why God gave different gifts and talents to man, and deposited in him various strengths and qualities that makes him unique, and utilize them to function effectively in certain jobs and careers that matched these strengths. Any endeavor in life that you often struggle with regardless of how long you've engaged in it, you seldom find the motivation to do the job, and seem not to be getting the desired satisfaction and fulfilment, that is clearly not the best for you and definitely not in conformity to your personality.

As a predominant sanguine personality, it's obvious that there are certain jobs and careers you cannot thrive in, or you will most likely struggle to achieve any remarkable success in them because you are deficient of the innate strengths and capabilities required to adequately and efficiently prosecute them. However, there are also other jobs that you're perfectly suitable for, which other temperaments may struggle with because they lack the requisite natural capabilities to be efficient in them. It is mainly the objective of this book, to highlight various innate strengths and capabilities you possess as a predominant sanguine perhaps with a blend of other temperaments, and the best jobs and careers they will aid you to be effortlessly and exceptionally successful in. As a sanguine, you've got enormous talents and qualities that can be deployed into certain career fields and as a result, make you the go-to person in that field. This is basically what this book is about, to expose these qualities and the best jobs or careers they're perfectly suitable for.

CHAPTER ONE

TEMPERAMENT AND VOCATION.

We are naturally gifted and endowed differently, and designed to function to our optimum capacity in various aspects of life. It is obviously not about our physical natural endowments; for the true making of a man is not just about his phenotypical appearance, but unarguably more about his genotypical content. Therefore, our natural endowments is more credibly measured by our cognitive and intellectual capabilities which are deeply rooted in the particular temperament we are born with. The theory of humorism as explained by the famous Greek physician Hippocrates, categorized the traits and behavioral patterns of every human being into four different categories, which are called the, <u>temperaments</u>. The temperament that we are born with, as a result of the genes and chromosomes that were transferred to us by our parents, and even much more from our grandparents during our conception, for a certainty make up our genotypical content. It is basically what influences and controls to a considerable extent what we can and cannot do. How we function in life, and do things, and to what extent we will succeed in various endeavors of life is determined by the influence of our temperament on us. Thus, since it is resident in the blood, and all the cells and organs that controls that part of our brain that's responsible for our cognitive and intellectual capabilities are linked to it, it will be logical to say that the temperaments we are born with will no doubt be so powerful in determining how cognitively and intellectually efficient we will be in different fields of endeavors in life. It's basically for this reason that in this chapter, we want to consider how our temperament relates to vocation. Or how the particular temperament we are born with naturally makes us attracted to certain vocations, and become so efficient and exceptional at them more than others are. But let us first of all understand what a vocation is.

> "We can't all be good at the same thing but we can all be better at different things".

What Is A Vocation?

According to the highest book in the world, which is the Holy Bible, a vocation simply means a natural calling. Ephesians 4:1. But majority of the dictionary interpretations use it synonymously with profession or career. Ideally speaking, it's unarguably who or what we are naturally (vocation wise) called to be or to do in life without too much struggle or dissipating so much effort to be very efficient in it. You could call it a natural talent or gift that you have to develop by practice, and with very little training and minimal effort, you will surely become high-flying in it. A vocation is not the skill or competence you gained through so many years of some rigorous trainings and practice in a particular field until you attained a glorious status in that field. That could best be described as your career or profession. Invariably, any skill gained or acquired through consistent trainings and practice in order to attain a certain level of professional competency in that particular field will best be described as a profession or career rather than vocation.

For instance, anyone could go through the rigorous training of becoming a medical doctor and perhaps finally becomes one, but not every doctor has the basic natural qualities and attributes that will enable them to efficiently practice the profession and become very efficient in it. Some even end up abandoning the profession maybe because they aren't enjoying the practice to concentrate on other endeavors they are more attracted to. Perhaps, it is the reason so many people aren't enjoying their job, and others have become very mechanical about it, but are willing to stay put in the job since it pays their bills. But as the day goes, and awareness level increases, more people will discover that they are ill-fated for the job or career path they have chosen. It is bad enough to be without a job, but it is even worse to have the wrong job that rarely make you feel somewhat fulfilled and satisfied, and always have to struggle to do it.

Differences Between Vocation And Profession Or Career:

Vocation is more profound, detailed, and very comprehensive. It is basically those innate capabilities or qualities that usually enables us to be effortlessly highly efficient and exceptional in certain career or professional path. In your profession or career, skillfulness and competence are usually acquired through undergoing some trainings, consistent practice, and perhaps years of experience. But a vocation is what you are innately equipped to do, and you naturally possess all the capabilities to be overwhelmingly successful in it. You may find your career or profession to be a bit clumsy at some point in practice and perhaps become mechanical about it, but the right vocation for you will usually be done so effortlessly and seamlessly with little to no difficulty.

In a career or profession, you certainly have to put in a lot of time and so much effort to undergo some trainings, and also practice very hard to achieve professional career success. But you will require minimum amount of effort to make a very remarkable impact in the right vocation that is suitable for your personality. Vocation is basically what you were well designed or created to do in life, having been naturally equipped with the capacity to do it. But a profession has to do with the skills and competence you gained while undergoing trainings in a particular field. Finally, a profession is usually more about acquired or learnt skills, more often than not through formal training. While a vocation consists mainly of some naturally inherent skills and abilities that will aid you to succeed in certain endeavors in life without much struggle. No human being is created empty. We are all naturally equipped and loaded by our creator (God), who is our manufacturer with some very distinct qualities and capabilities to accomplish remarkable things in various fields of life.

As human beings, we are naturally designed to function in a way that creatively adds value to what we do, or have consistently been doing for a long time. If you keep on doing a particular thing repeatedly and keep getting the same type of result though it could be a positive expected result, but as long as you are not creatively adding value to that outcome or result, then it is obviously an indication that you are not improving or advancing. In more specific or clearer terms, a job or career path that we find it difficult to be creative in, or can seamlessly deploy our creativity in order to add value to it after many years of practice is obviously not the best for us, surely not our calling, and of course not our vocation. For the right vocation for our personality, will in the long run make us become more creative, highly productive, continuously advancing, and will certainly bring about a very satisfactory feeling.

The human brain is designed in a way that it has the capacity to receive and assimilate anything that is consistently given to it. It is of course for this reason that anyone could be trained to become so skilled, competent, and a professional in any field of life. But not everyone for sure possesses the natural capabilities, competencies, and qualities to become exceptional in those fields or make a mark in them. Therefore, knowing and discovering the right kind of vocation for your personality and being so intentionally insistent on walking worthy of it, will for sure help you to stand out from the crowd and make an indelible positive impact in that field. Having said that, let us consider how temperament relates to vocation, or link the between temperament and vocation.

How Does Temperament Relate To Vocation?

Our temperament are as a result of those genotypical genes and chromosomes that were naturally transferred to us during our conception. Since it is in our DNA, and it's also connected to that part of our brain (cerebrum) that controls intelligence or our intellectual capacity, reasoning, cognitive ability, behavioral patterns and tendencies which make us very unique and distinct from others. It is therefore not unimaginable for it to also determine and influence our natural vocational strengths, qualities, and capabilities. As mentioned earlier, there are four basic categories of temperaments, which of course influences to a very large extent the attitude and behavioral patterns of every human being and also determines the personality traits of the carriers of any of these four temperament types.

A carrier of the sanguine temperament has its own traits and behavioral pattern, and will naturally possess some capabilities or qualities, which we can also refer to as the "strengths of the sanguine" temperament. These strengths and qualities of a sanguine are markedly different from those of the choleric, melancholy and phlegmatic. Even though there may be some similarities in certain areas, but it is usually at varying degrees. Basically, it is these strengths and qualities that points us to the vocation that is best and right for us, for which we are designed to function effectively in, and of course become high-flying. Just the same way the corresponding weaknesses of each of them make us to be quite inefficient in certain vocations, and rarely exceptional in them. Therefore, the link between our temperament and the right vocation, are the natural strengths and weaknesses that are associated with, and inherent in the temperament we are born with.

Our natural temperament strengths are basically what should determine the right vocation for our personality type. For those are the strengths or qualities that will help us to be unlaborious in our pursuit of success in our chosen career path and profession. It is undoubtedly for this reason that there are certain jobs or careers that a predominant sanguine personality will be very efficient in, which a melancholy will struggle with, or become ill-fated for. Because the former possessed some basic natural qualities that will for sure enable him to without much exertion of energy overwhelmingly succeed in those jobs or careers. And in some careers a predominant melancholy will be exceptionally efficient in, a sanguine will be ill-fated for them, and will rarely be successful in them. The four basic temperaments possess natural strengths and qualities that makes us unique and distinct and these strengths ought to point us to the right vocation that's suitable for our personality. But it is so unfortunate that so many people are not so intentional about insisting on the right vocation that matched their temperament strengths and qualities. Consequently, they struggle to be efficient in their job, and will rarely make any remarkable positive impact in it. But insisting on a job, career, or profession that is very consistent with our temperament strengths will for sure make us high-flying in our job.

CHAPTER TWO

DISCOVERING YOUR VOCATIONAL COMPETENCIES.

> "Your personality and vocation are inseparable, both must align to make you feel fulfilled and satisfied".

Human beings are naturally equipped with become exceptional in However, it is not created equally, but are different abilities to whatever they do. uncommon that we could be multi-talented, thus be able to do different things. But there must always be that one particular thing that we can do so well and better than the next person, and we will also rarely struggle getting it done. The temperament and blends of it that we are born with is innately inundated with various strengths and abilities to enable us efficiently discharge our duties in various aspects of life, and effortlessly accomplish certain tasks that others may struggle with, since they are naturally deficient of these strengths and abilities that are necessary to perfectly get them accomplished. It's mainly for this reason that we need to know the particular temperament category we belong, and also have a perfect understanding of its innate strengths and abilities in order to know the right vocation we are best fitted for. Temperament is our inherited traits, it is responsible for the natural way we are designed to function in life, that is undoubtedly different from the next person. Each of the four temperament types is accompanied by various strengths and weaknesses which always reflects in the personality traits and behavioral patterns of different persons. While the strengths enables us to without much struggle succeed in many different endeavors in life, the weaknesses usually inhibits or attempts to scuttle the chances of our success.

Our vocation is our calling, it is what we are created or born to do in life, and of course do it better than the other person. It is therefore very imperative that before deciding on a career path that we want to undertake in life or maybe the vocation we want to practice and walk worthy of, we should endeavor to first of all understand ourself by discovering the temperament we are born with, and its corresponding strengths and weaknesses. For this will enable us to realize the best career fields and professions that aligned with our basic temperament strengths and those that are incongruous to it. For next to being unemployed, the worst and most exasperating thing that can befall a person is to have the wrong job or be in the wrong vocation. It is so unbelievable how many people in contemporary time despise their job or the work they are doing. No wonder it becomes debilitating and suchlike drudgery to them because they lack the motivation, passion and enthusiasm for the job. As technology advances and awareness level increases, increasing number of persons will certainly realize that they are ill-fated and unfit for the career path they have chosen. For majority of the jobs, particularly unskilled and some semi-skilled jobs would have been automated out of existence, and it will be required by organizations and industries to deploy your natural capabilities to efficiently do your job. Therefore, it's absolutely very important that you become intentional about the career path you want to take in life, or the vocation you want to consider practicing.

It's bad enough to be without a job because apart from being financially bankrupt, you also lack the opportunity to be productive or work productively. But even worse than being without a job, is to find oneself in a job or career that makes one unproductive, thus, leaves us unfulfilled and dissatisfied. It is extremely frustrating to be found in such careers or jobs. There is nothing as gratifying and invigorating as having a job that makes you work productively, and you don't have to be mechanical about it. Little wonder so many persons have to change their job countless number of times because they are not getting that desired satisfaction and fulfilment from it. But just changing jobs or perhaps moving from one job to another cannot guarantee you that fulfilment and satisfaction, until you are able to discover the secret of finding the right job that suits your personality.

One of the surest way to avoid vocational frustration or feeling like a round peg in a square hole, is to know your temperament and blends of it, and its natural vocational capabilities. Then, you become deliberate about finding a job or vocation that allows you to express your natural temperament qualities and attributes. When it comes to deciding on a life time job or career, one of the factor one must consider is choosing the one that ranks even with ones natural temperament strengths and qualities in order to avoid making a career mistake. The benefits of insisting on a career that is completely in conformity with your primary temperament strengths are enormous and absolutely rewarding. You will not only have the right motivation and inspiration to always want to do the job, you will also feel some sort of fulfilment and satisfaction any time you engage in it. We want to consider six major ways of finding the right job or career that is suitable for your personality, courtesy of your natural vocational strengths and capabilities.

6 Ways To Find The Right Job That Suits Your Personality:

In this chapter, we want to outline and consider in detail six major steps to discovering your natural vocational competencies that will enable you to without much struggle or expending so much energy become successful in certain jobs and careers that are suitable for your temperament type.

1. Know Your Temperament:

You cannot find the right career that suits or matches your personality, and subsequently gives you the expected satisfaction unless you know and understand who you are. The sum total of who you are, or the real you is embedded in your personality, and which also no doubt emanates from your inherited temperament. However you act or behave, even how you do your job, the type of attitude you bring to bare on it, be it positive or negative, all can be traced to the temperament you're born with. If you are so conversant with the temperaments, by just watching how someone behaves or acts, and their attitude to things, and even how they work, you can easily tell correctly the careers that they will be best suited for. The temperament we are born with rarely changes, it follows us all through life. Although parenting and parental upbringing, education, societal or environmental influences or other factors may try to tweak it a bit, but it really does not change it. As we will often unconsciously continue to yield to its influences on us.

It's basically for this reason that you need to be aware of the temperament you are born with, and its influence on you. It will help you to understand your personality, and why you act and behave, or do some of the things you do. It will no doubt also help you to be your real self, live according to your personality, without being so much hard on, or critical of yourself. Knowing who you are, simply means understanding your personality. That is, how you function or operate as an individual. You've got to understand the fact that you're different from the other person, not really in terms of physical looks per say, but in capabilities and deficiencies, and also in terms of your strengths and weaknesses. You definitely need to realize that there are some things that you can naturally do better than the other person, and there are others you will most likely often struggle with, and which the next person will be better at. It could also be things you are so much passionate about, that often arouses your interest, but could also be irritating to the other person. These diversities in our traits, interests, and how we do things, makes everyone unique as individuals. Consequently, this uniqueness is naturally embedded in our inherited temperaments. Thus, since our temperament determines our personality, and influences everything we do in life. It is therefore necessary that we are aware of the temperament we are born with, so we could be able to function optimally to the best of our ability in any career field we find ourselves. It's for this reason that knowing your temperament is the first step to finding or discovering the right career that matched your personality.

2. Understand And Analyze Your Temperament Strengths and Weaknesses:

The four basic temperament categories of **Sanguine, Choleric, Melancholy,** and **Phlegmatic** have got inherent weaknesses and strengths. And it's these strengths and weaknesses that will enable you to figure out some of the best career fields you can function optimally, and also be a guide to finding the right job or career that matches your temperament strengths, so that you'll be able to function very effectively in that job or career. The strengths and qualities of a predominant sanguine person will often endear him to some careers, and no doubt enable him to function effectively in them, while such careers could irritate a predominant melancholy and he will fail woefully in them. But the typical sanguine weakness will rarely allow him to succeed in some careers that a typical melancholy person will be very successful in.

For instance, it will be very difficult for a predominant sanguine person to become a medical doctor, and succeed in the medical profession. Because he lacks that discipline and concentration to go through the rigors of medical school, neither does he have the meticulousness to practice the profession. While a predominant melancholy or even phlegmatic will do very well as a medical doctor, because they've got that discipline to go through medical school, and also the carefulness, detailed, and thoroughness to succeed in the career. However, they will most likely fail in career like salesmanship and marketing, because they lack charisma and liveliness, plus people-oriented qualities to convince anyone to pander to what they are marketing or selling, which is basically where the core strengths of a predominant sanguine is domicile.

It's more often for this reason that so many persons decides to abandon whatever they had studied in college or university and go into, or focus on other formal or informal career fields in life. While those who often decides to stick with careers that are not relevant to their temperament strengths are rarely productive or successful in them and sometimes, they lament for all of their years in such careers, because they aren't getting that fulfilment and satisfaction they desire. It's basically for this reason that you have to choose a career path that is in agreement with your primary and secondary temperament strengths, where you will be able to function to the best of your ability. And one of the way you can be sure that you are on the right career path that is relevant to your temperament strengths, is to first, know your temperament. Secondly, you've got to understand and analyze the strength and weaknesses that are inherent in your temperament. You may have to list them, to enable you figure out some of the careers that will match your strengths, and those that your weaknesses may hinder or prevent you from performing effectively in them.

3. Make A List Of All The Careers You'd Like To Go Into:

After identifying all the weaknesses and strengths inherent in your temperament, and perhaps had list them down. The next thing you've got to do, is to make a list of all the careers you'd want to go into, whether they're in the formal or informal sector. As a teenager who may be planning to go into high school for the first time, this is not just important, but it's also very reassuring that you know what you want. Even as a high school leaver, college graduate or an adult who may probably be confused about the right career path to take in life, listing all the careers you'd love to venture into is very necessary in order to enable you figure out which career path that will be best suitable for you. It's possible that we could make a list of all these careers, based on our selfish desire, how big they sound, or how financially rewarding they may be. But don't worry, just list them. Very soon you will discover if they are the best for your personality or not.

4. Know What It Requires To Undergo The Trainings In Those Careers And Be Successful In Them:

Different careers often requires different training methodologies that are specific to them. The trainings required to produce a medical doctor cannot be the same as that required to produce a lawyer, even though both of them are required to go through the same formal education. For medicine and surgery is pure science, while the law profession is basically art related. Similarly, to become a professional footballer, the trainings you'd go through will be different from that of a professional tennis, golf or baseball player, though they are all in the same sports category. Every career has got specific training methodologies that are no doubt peculiar to them. And unless you go through the right training, you definitely cannot become a professional in that field. It's basically for this reason that you need to know what it requires to successfully go through the training in those careers you have listed, in order to become very good and efficient in them. For all formal careers, going to college or university, and getting a degree will be very necessary. While for the informal careers, acquiring the basic requisite skills may just be enough to help you succeed. But prior to getting a college or university degree, or deciding on getting an informal skill, you definitely need to do little introspection into your basic natural temperament strengths and weaknesses, in order to choose the right career that match your temperament strengths and discard the ones that will impede your success in them as a result of the weaknesses in your temperament.

For instance a predominant sanguine naturally lacks self-discipline and focus, thus, there are some careers that requires these natural qualities for you to be successful in them. Similarly, melancholy and phlegmatic personalities lacks charisma and liveliness, thus they may find it difficult succeeding in careers that these qualities are needed. While for the typical choleric personality, he lacks empathy and humanitarianism, and like his sanguine counterpart, hates too much details and analysis, therefore, will definitely find it hard succeeding in careers that requires these qualities to be successful in them. It's for this reason that before enrolling for a particular training or course to acquire a skill or perhaps obtain a degree you've got to analyze your temperament strengths to know if you've got the requisite strengths or qualities that will enable you to succeed in that career.

5. Consider Your Secondary Temperament:

Much as we make emphasis on our primary or predominant temperament, it is also very important that we are aware of our secondary temperament and give consideration to it. Everyone has got a blend of two or more temperaments, which we of course refer to as the temperament blends. It is very rare for anyone to be completely or 100 percent sanguine, choleric, melancholic, and phlegmatic without a blend of any other temperament. But there is always one which predominates the rest, because its blend ratio or blend percentage is higher in amount compared to others. And this is basically what we refer to as our primary or predominant temperament, while the others are our secondary temperament. For instance, someone could be 70 percent sanguine and 30 percent phlegmatic. For this person, he will possess more strengths or qualities of a sanguine, and less of a typical phlegmatic. Consequently he will also more often be influenced by his predominant sanguine temperament, and will occasionally behave like a phlegmatic.

Knowing your secondary temperament is as important as knowing your primary or predominant temperament. Because it will enable you to have different career choices and diversify into other careers that are relevant to your primary and secondary temperament strengths. You could discover that the natural strengths and qualities of your predominant temperament may not be sufficient for you to go into a particular career and be successful in it, but when you check your secondary temperament, you'd discover that those strengths and qualities are within reach, and are naturally blended to help you succeed in that career, especially if the blend ratio is, 60:40 or maybe 55:45. Temperament blend enables us to function effectively in different career fields, areas or departments. For instance, predominant sanguine may not have self-discipline, but if his second temperament is melancholic, he will be a bit more disciplined. Similarly, a melancholic may be low in confidence or has got poor self-esteem, but if perhaps his secondary temperament is say, choleric or sanguine in substantial amount, he will be a bit more confident and charismatic. This is how our temperament blend shapes our personality and impacts us in different areas of life. Therefore, you need to give equal amount of consideration and attention to your secondary temperament like you often do to your primary temperament, and also consider its strengths and qualities when trying to choose a career path in life. This is so that you will have more career options, and also maximize the strengths inherent in both temperaments.

6. Match Your Temperament Strengths To The Careers You've Listed:

If you had figured out the natural strengths associated with your primary and secondary temperament, then it's time to do the practical task of matching these strengths and qualities with the relevant careers that you had listed, to see the ones that matched at least, 80 percent of your strengths. In some careers you may have a blend of both your primary and secondary temperament strengths, perhaps in ratio of 70:30, 60:40 or 55:45 to help you make the right career choice. For instance, if you like to go into the sales and marketing career, your primary temperament ought to be sanguine or choleric, because these two temperaments have got the expressiveness, charisma, word-of-mouth, and the people-oriented qualities to succeed in this career. But a melsan temperament blend of 60:40 could also succeed in sales and marketing career even though his first temperament is melancholic. But because of the secondary sanguine temperament, he will most likely succeed in it. Similarly, a career such as accounting will bore a typical sanguine or choleric, because it requires attention to details, keep up with daily routines, record keeping, and dealing with so much figures, or calculations, which these temperament lacks. But if they were say, a Sanphleg or Cholphleg, maybe of 60:40 or 55:45 blend ratio, they may do better in the accounting career, since they've also got phlegmatic as the secondary temperament.

Every career has specific strengths that are relevant to it. And these strengths are often embedded in our inherited temperaments or blends of it. When you've known your temperament and perhaps temperament blends, with its inherent weaknesses and strengths. The next thing is to understand the strengths and qualities it takes to succeed in different career fields, then match each of them to careers you have listed. If you can get five out of seven, or six out of eight strengths that are relevant to succeed in a particular career, then you've discovered your career path in life. It's also possible that you could get three or four strengths from your primary or predominant temperament, and another three from your secondary, strengths of the two different temperaments will also combine to enable you succeed in some careers that you may find very difficult succeeding in, if you've got just one type of temperament type. But rarely does anyone have just one type of temperament, it's often a blend of two or more. And this is why you must know and understand both your predominant and secondary temperaments with their innate strengths and weaknesses.

CHAPTER THREE

NATURAL VOCATIONAL STRENGTHS OF A PREDOMINANT SANGUINE PERSONALITY.

WHAT ARE NATURALLY SANGUINES GOOD AT?

> "Sanguines are like air, seem too common and always available for everyone but quite indispensable for human existence".

The sanguine personality is a very talented and gifted person, and the world is blessed and enriched with these air personalities. These personalities have so far benefited the world very immensely with their happy-charisma, and people-oriented qualities which makes interpersonal relationships so easy and seamless. Despite their natural weaknesses and oddities, the sanguine is unarguably the go-to person when it comes to human interpersonal relationship, and he is more like a bridge builder who often connects, links, and brings different people together. For his natural selflessness and congeniality makes him a very attractive person that so many people usually find it very easy and comfortable to relate with him even just within a short period of meeting him. Regardless of the fact that he is a natural attention seeker and flamboyant person, but he is the most selfless and light-hearted when it comes to interpersonal relationship. The typical sanguine personality is very gifted and talented in diverse ways, but it is quite unfortunate that majority of them lacks the self-discipline, resoluteness, and consistency to harness and unleash their potentials, and appropriately channel them into very meaningful and profitable ventures that will benefit them and others. It is basically for this reason that in this chapter, we want to consider 9 basic things that the predominant sanguine personality is innately very good at, for which he can channel all his energy towards, and make his natural skill and talent come to bare on his endeavors in life.

9 Basic Things A Typical Sanguine Personality Is Naturally Good At:

It should be clearly stated that those basic tasks, jobs or personal endeavors that we often have passion for, derive inner joyful feeling from, and find very fulfilling and satisfying whenever we do or engage in them regardless of any instant financial gratification that comes from doing them, are basically the things we are naturally and exceptionally good at. And no one else can do them better than we do. Let's look at these nine major things that a typical sanguine is naturally very good at that no other temperament can measure up to him in these areas.

1. Talking:

Although some people may consider this as a weakness, it is relative, and depends on your standpoint. However, it may be agreeable to some extent especially when the talking becomes unreasonable. But one fact you cannot take away from a typical sanguine personality is that, he is a very good talker. He can talk for a very long time without getting tired, for as long as he's got someone listening to him. None among the other basic temperaments come close to the talking energy and capacity of a sanguine. His mouth is his strength, and he can use it to get the attention of anyone and keep the person indulged, listening to him for a very long time. The sanguine is never in want of what to say at any given time, and you will often wonder how he manages to conjure up what to say at any point in time, and if he actually prepared for it. However, he may sometimes talk amiss if he is carried away, or maybe under the influence of his emotions. But if he can regulate himself and be more decorous in his speeches and talking ability then he will be a much better talker that everyone will love listening to. Therefore, if you need someone who can keep people engaged for a long time with his natural talking ability without getting them bored, then a typical sanguine is the perfect person that qualify for, and suits that particular role. And as a predominant sanguine person, rather than allow your ability to talk to become a weakness, you can turn it into a strength by using it for some better and more profitable ventures like; marketing and sales, **voice-over art**, **podcasting**, audiobook production, and any other profitable jobs or venture that requires being able to talk for a long time.

2. Socializing:

If there is any temperament that knows how to easily adapt to a new environment quickly, identify with the people there, and become accustomed to their way of life, it's the typical sanguine personality. He doesn't find it hard to socialize, and interact with everyone he meets in his new address. His natural charisma, plus his people-oriented qualities usually enables him to seamlessly work his way through the hearts of people and become acquainted with them within a short time of his stay or sojourn in a new place. No other temperament does this better than the predominant sanguine. A typical introvert melancholy or phlegmatic will rather wait for you to come to him first, and seek him out for friendship, while a typical choleric is usually self-sufficient enough that he rarely has the time to meet or know you. But a typical sanguine is sure going to come to you, even if you don't. It's for this reason that he may succeed in an ambassadorial job or career, missionary work, or any job that requires creating relationship with new sets of people in a different place or environment.

3. Meeting New People:

There's no other temperament that enjoys meeting, interacting, and relating with new people or new sets of people in an unfamiliar place more than a predominant sanguine personality. In fact, he usually finds his meaning and a sense of satisfaction and fulfilment in life when he comes in contact with new people, where he uses his humor and flamboyance to freely express himself and keep them fascinated. He does not find it difficult to make new friends wherever he is, and he's the only temperament that is not in want of friends, for he's got them in very large numbers. Typical melancholies and phlegmatics will clearly be initially too shy, uncharismatic, or perhaps egocentric to be the first to seek you out for friendship or an interpersonal relationship, but will usually wait for you to make that first move. While a typical choleric person will be too busy to even notice you, even if he does, he's so self-sufficient and reliant to need you, unless he's got something he can use you to accomplish. But the sanguine personality is so selfless and people-centric that he rarely care being the first to initiate a conversation and relationship with you. It's basically for this reason that he usually succeeds in client and customer service representative, sales and marketing jobs, and some receptionist duties.

4. Public Speaking:

Asides the choleric personality who comes close, no other temperament is better than a predominant sanguine in facing a crowd of people, and speak to them in the most humorous, fascinating and attention grabbing manner without boring his audience or inducing sleep in them. A typical sanguine person is so charismatic that he is rarely fidgety on seeing a multitude of people. He seldom get frightened or shy when he is called upon to speak to a gathering of people. In fact, the more the crowd, the better motivated and confident he becomes about expressing his liveliness and flamboyance. He's an orator, who usually makes use of his oratory and fascinating storytelling ability to keep most of his audience or listeners fascinated and enthusiastic about his speech. It's basically for this reason that he's more often hired to speak in most conferences, seminars, talk shows, symposiums, political campaigns, and any other gathering where there will be high number of people attending, who are expecting a mix of motivational speaking and funfair. No one knows how to make use of different gesticulations, illustrations, and storytelling to crave the indulgence of his audience more than a typical sanguine personality. Therefore, public speaking jobs or career is one of the best that a sanguine can channel his talking energy to, because he is naturally a very good public speaker.

5. Entertainment:

There's clearly no way we can talk about the entertainment sector without making mention of a typical sanguine personality, because he is a natural entertainer, the life of the party who do not find it hard to WOW his audience and make the entertainment or event arena so lively and fun. He is naturally a very creatively hilarious and lively person who seamlessly make his creativity come alive in his ability to lift up your mood through entertainment. There's no other temperament that is more gifted and talented in the art of making people laugh, and creatively entertain them more than a predominant sanguine. Performing music arts, comic acting, dancing, and any other activity that requires creatively coming up with new concept that could induce excitement and high emotional ecstasy in others, are doubtlessly some of his major areas of strengths and ability in the entertainment sector.

6. Masters Of Ceremony, MC:

You certainly cannot take this away from a typical sanguine personality. No other type of temperament is naturally more adept at crafting and creating some kind of jokes and fairy tales that usually makes people laugh at different interludes of a ceremony or an event than the typical sanguine person. He knows how to combine his natural sense of humor, creativity, and storytelling ability to make everyone relish the occasion. At times, he makes use of the things he sees around him to create an interesting story line that makes the guests laugh, or emote a feeling of excitement in them. Sometimes the story might not be too interesting, but he usually uses his creativity to make it look more interesting than it really is. Thus if you need a very efficient Master of Ceremony for any of your occasion, you should consider hiring typical sanguine personality, or at least someone whose secondary temperament is sanguine, because he is the perfect person for that role.

7. Creative Writing & Storytelling:

Apart from a melancholy who comes close, no other temperament is gifted with the art of fiction book writing more than a typical sanguine personality. His natural creative and imaginative ability usually enables him to effortlessly conceptualize thoughts and ideas that could make for a good and interesting storyline or book. But a typical sanguine needs to be more disciplined and composed, in order to succeed in fiction book writing. If a predominant sanguine can be a lot more self-disciplined, consistent, organized, and willing to deploy his creative writing ability, he'll be a very successful fiction book writer and achieve a lot more in the creative writing aspect of the entertainment sector.

8. Sports:

Even though this is not exclusive to a typical sanguine personality alone, since sports or success in sporting events and other type of physical activities and exercise could also be learnt and acquired as a skill through consistent practice. But a predominant sanguine is of course one of those that is naturally gifted and talented in various sporting activities. His natural enthusiasm and expressiveness usually enables him to succeed in sports or go farther ahead in any sporting activity he chooses than others. He's arguably the only temperament that naturally possess a spirit of sportsmanship without seeing the game as a do or die affair. He knows how to motivate himself to do better next time if peradventure he loses out in any sporting competition. It's unlike his phlegmatic and melancholy counterparts who may become depressed and will need some motivation and morale boosting to be able to come back to their best. Or a choleric who will become so angry and paranoid with everyone if he loses a game. But the typical sanguine knows how to encourage other team mates and himself, and accept his loss while hoping to comeback stronger next time.

9. Art Works:

The natural creativity of the predominant sanguine personality is often accentuated when it comes to arts, and production of various art works. Art is basically a type of unstructured work that usually expresses feelings, emotions, and vision. Example are painting, architecture, sculptures, drawing, literature, calligraphy, photography, motion pictures, print making, music, performing, theatre, dance etc. To be successful in any of these art work or activity requires being creative, expressive, and also putting your feelings and emotions into what you are trying to create, which ought to be natural and be emotionally appealing to people. Of course, since all predominant sanguines are naturally creative and expressive type of people who often easily expresses their feelings and emotions, they will not find it difficult succeeding in art, and production of art works if they channel their energy in that direction.

In conclusion, regardless of their natural <u>temperament weaknesses and oddities</u>, predominant sanguine personalities are no doubt among the most gifted and talented of the four temperament categories. But lack of self-discipline, poor organization and also their overindulgence more often than not hinder them from tapping into their innate gifts and talents, or scuttles their chances of achieving personal success in endeavors that are tied to their temperament strength and abilities. But if sanguines can be very intentional about looking inwards, and be disciplined enough, they've got enormous amount of natural talents and abilities that can be maximized in order to achieve very remarkable success in their field of work and endeavors. Any job, career, or activity that directly impacts positively on the life of others, and make them happy and elated is basically what a predominant sanguine is innately excellent at, and he will of course get enormous amount of satisfactory feeling and fulfilment from doing them.

CHAPTER FOUR

MAXIMIZING YOUR VOCATIONAL STRENGTHS AS A SANGUINE.

> "A gift not used for its rightful purpose is useless".

To sound more like a broken record, different temperaments has got peculiar strengths that serves or suits various career purposes, and also weaknesses that tends to hinder the actualization of such purposes and intents if allowed to hold sway. If you're conversant with the various temperaments and their peculiarities, you will agree with me that the strength and weaknesses of a sanguine are quite different from those of the choleric. And also the melancholy's strengths and weaknesses differs from those of the phlegmatics, despite the fact that they belong to the same extrovert and introvert categories respectively. However, there could be some similarities in their individual strengths and weaknesses depending on their proximity to each other. Do not also forget that an individual could have a combination of two or more temperaments embedded in them when this happens, they will naturally possess a combination of both the strengths and weaknesses of all those temperaments combined in them, which will usually be in varying proportions. This will be a topic for another day. But in our discussion in this chapter, we want to look at how to maximize your primary temperament strength to achieve success in your career.

What Is Career Success?

Career success simply means to attain financial stability while doing the job that makes you happy and feel very fulfilled. When your job makes you feel elated and accomplished that you desire to get stuck with it, it clearly means that, that job concurs with your personality or temperament. The question then is, how do you attain financial success and stability in your career doing what you love? This is precisely what we want to discuss in this chapter. It's basically to share with you how to maximize your basic or primary temperament strengths to achieve career success and become financially stable. If your predominant temperament is sanguine or choleric, melancholy or phlegmatic there are core strengths that are associated with each of them that could be harnessed, and also maximized to enable you become exceptional in your chosen career field regardless of the fact that you could possess other secondary strengths.

What Is Vocational Strengths In Temperament?

Straight off, vocational strengths in temperament refers to those natural strengths that are associated with our temperament type that enables us to become exceptional in certain vocations where these basic strengths and qualities are in demand. Temperament is everything; for inside it, are some natural strengths and qualities that are peculiar to each of them. The four temperament types are accompanied by various innate strengths and corresponding weaknesses. But for the purpose of this chapter, we want to focus on the strengths alone which enables the carriers of any of these temperament to be better at certain vocations, or effortlessly succeed in some jobs and career path more than others. But more specifically in this book, we are interested in the sanguine temperament and some of the major strengths associated with it that enables the sanguine personality to be head and shoulder above others in certain vocations.

Therefore, since temperament is everything because it influences almost everything we do in life and how we do them. The strengths and weaknesses linked to each temperament is undoubtedly responsible for our personality, and to a very large extent describes who we are. As the strengths enables us to easily navigate through life and without dissipating so much effort and energy be able to succeed in certain career fields and also become exceptional in fields that aligned with our temperament strengths, so also the weaknesses are there to scuttle our success and hinder us from becoming efficient and productive in life. Therefore, since our natural temperament strengths are potent enough to enable us easily navigate through life and be exceptional in what we do, then it won't be out of place to refer to it as our common natural gift that are given to us to function effectively and efficiently in life.

However, it's perplexing how many people intentionally or unintentionally refuse to maximize their natural gift to enable them become effortlessly and exceptionally successful in jobs that aligned with these gifts. While some despise their natural gifts and talents because they consider them to be too negligible, and others because of challenges of unemployment, and ignorance of the importance of personally maximizing their innate gifts and be sought after by others, consequently make them go through life without making any positive impact. Hence, they find it so easy to go into other fields that they are not designed to function in, thus becoming very redundant and unproductive in those fields. The reason why we are given a natural gift and talent is to maximize it, make it become very useful not just to us alone but to others as well. A gift not used is useless, and can be abused. In similar way, a natural gift that is not maximized is not only useless, but the generosity of the giver has been wasted and made mockery of. It is quite unfortunate that a lot of people are unknowingly making God look stupid by not utilizing or by despising the natural gifts given to them by Him. Matthew 25:15-26.

How Do You Maximize Your Temperament Strength For Career Success As A Sanguine?

There are no hard and fast rules to harnessing and maximizing your primary temperament strength for career success and financial stability. The rule of thumb here is "practice makes perfect". To become perfect at what you do, the generally accepted truth is that you ought to consistently practice and improve yourself in that thing. As a predominant sanguine, you've no doubt inherited some of these strengths at birth, courtesy of the basic temperament you're born with. Having inherited them, it's very unwise to sit back and relax without utilizing them or perhaps use them in very uncomely and unproductive manner that does not bring any substance to you personally or impact positively on your career.

For instance as a sanguine, instead of building and improving on your natural eloquence and salesmanship ability by enrolling in some effective communication and customer service and relationship courses to further enhance and maximize these strengths, you decide to always engage it chit-chatting, irresponsible and unreasonable talking which clearly does not add any value to your life and career. You can choose to maximize your natural gift or temperament strengths by reading books on effective communication, enrolling for some effective communication classes, sales and marketing classes, going for courses in the entertainment sector, and finally insisting on getting a job or working in fields that matched your natural vocational temperament strengths or gifts. This will for sure help you to sharpen these natural gifts, maximize your temperament strengths and qualities, and become more productive and efficient.

CHAPTER FIVE

BEST JOBS AND CAREERS FOR A PREDOMINANT SANGUINE PERSONALITY.

As a typical sanguine, career is best for you, or you take in life. Don't you in this chapter some best describes your

"You don't become the best in a field by doing your best, you become the best in a field by aligning yourself with the best fields for you".

you may be asking which which career path should worry, I will be showing careers that suits, and personality as a

sanguine. Asking this question or reading this book is a clear signal that you already know who you are, and makes me believe that I am talking to the right person. Thus, it is needless to bore you further with the nitty-gritty of who a sanguine is. Of course, if you are also a regular reader of my blog posts, you should by now know who a sanguine is. But for the benefit of those who do not know or perhaps as a reminder, I think it is important we summarize and remind ourselves of who a predominant sanguine is, once more.

Straight off, sanguines are described as air, they are free and ubiquitous personalities at different times. They are super extroverts and the most outgoing of all the temperaments. They are very lively, expressive, charismatic, fun-loving, highly-spirited and people-oriented individuals, who could make you relish every minute spent with them, with their fascinating storytelling skills and ability. A sanguine is never shy or too timid to talk to anybody, and he will usually be the first to initiate a conversation. This character makes him easily attract friends and admirers who will not find it difficult sparing some of their time to give them audience. There's no other temperament that often attracts the attention of people more than typical sanguines. Therefore, for someone who epitomizes these qualities, what careers do you think is best him or her? It is a no brainer that careers that often brings them face to face with people, or people- oriented careers are the very best for sanguines. And they usually excel in such careers more than others.

As a sanguine, there are many other things you could do, but it's obviously in a career that makes you interface with people, that your strength lies. And you will no doubt effortlessly succeed in these careers and reach the top. While other temperaments may struggle to adapt or seamlessly do the job, you'll never struggle in these career fields because your primary temperament makes you a better fit for them. You've got people-oriented qualities, charisma and word-of-mouth to talk and convince anyone about anything, and make them actually buy into what you're proposing, especially if you've got choleric as your secondary temperament. This chapter will cover some of the best career opportunities you could venture into as a sanguine, the prospects in each of these careers are enormous. Because natural skills and talents alone may not suffice in this modern times, but they will doubtlessly enable you to effortlessly and overwhelmingly succeed in these career fields. Therefore, insisting on a career in these fields by enrolling in a formal training in them, you will be able to unleash your refined natural gifts for an outstanding success in these careers.

As a sanguine, there are a quite a good number of jobs you may be successful in, as long such jobs and careers gives you the leverage to meet and interface with different people. But the below careers fields were chosen based on the fact that they are the first that rank even with your predominant sanguine nature, very profitable with lots of prospects, and you've got the natural strengths already, to easily adapt and succeed in them because of the primary temperament you're born with.

For any predominant sanguine, the first career that should easily come to mind and which you should seriously consider is sales and marketing. This career is one of the best for you, and not just that, you'll feel very fulfilled and happy as you see your turnover and increased figure leads in sales. As a sanguine, you've got the word-of- mouth, charisma and congeniality to meet and talk to anyone and convince them to buy a product or patronize a service, which other temperaments may struggle to do. Converting your audience to paying customers and clients is not such a difficult task for you. Your core strength in this career, is your friendliness, the warm and convivial atmosphere you create with your audience. Which thus gives them the passion to listen to you.

The strategy you need to apply more in order to overwhelmingly succeed in this career is, make friends with people and build relationship first, before you sell to them. As long as new businesses keeps springing up, existing business and brands wants to increase their clientele and customer base, and get higher Return On Investment (ROI), these career is sure not going away anytime soon. You could be hired by emerging, existing, and already established brands to help them attract more clients and customers and increase their ROI. You could also start your own sales and marketing firm, and have these new businesses and brands outsource their marketing jobs to you. This is one career you'll definitely find very attractive as a sanguine.

Auctioneering:

If you have been to your local market center to witness how goods and merchandise are auctioned, you would agree with me that those auctioneers have enough charisma, humor, word of mouth, and light-heartedness to attract the attention of passersby, and increase their Salesforce. No other temperament naturally possess these qualities more than a predominant sanguine. For they enable him to be the best salesman who does not find it difficult to quickly auction his goods without much struggle. It is basically for this reason that no other temperament is a better auctioneer than a predominant sanguine personality.

Entertainment(Acting & Music):

Careers in the entertainment sector, particularly comic acting and performing music, is also another career path that's very attractive to sanguines. Most sanguine finds careers in the entertainment industry very intriguing. Since you're naturally an outgoing and people-oriented personality, who loves to make and see people happy, and also make them feel your style and persona. Succeeding in this career will not be an uphill task for you. You could leverage on this strength to go into the entertainment industry and prove your worth. However, as a sanguine, you're not a good songwriter or music composer unless you've got melancholy as your secondary temperament. You can buy and read books that will enable you to improve your songwriting skills. As long as human beings likes to be entertained, feel relaxed and happy, a career in the entertainment sector is sure one lucrative career that will never go away.

Public Relations & Marketing:

Sanguines often makes excellent public relations, branding and also marketing officers. Because of their ability to relate well with people and use their oratory and sugar-coated tongues to launder the image of anyone or the organization they work for. Therefore, if you're a typical sanguine or you've got sanguine as your predominant temperament, I think you should consider starting a career in public relations and marketing. You will without much struggle succeed in this career field since you're already a people's person and you've got the charisma and word-of-mouth to make people believe in what you endorse and propose. You could get hired by top brands and organizations to help launder their image, and market their brands. Even politicians could hire you for image laundering and marketing.

Public Speaking:

Every successful motivational public speaker must have some sanguine traits in them. For the task of facing and standing before a crowd of people to speak in a fascinating and most interesting way to them, especially for the first time requires the natural happy-charisma of the sanguine, plus a little courage and self-confidence of the choleric, if choleric were to be your secondary temperament. As someone who's predominantly sanguine by temperament, you will no doubt be head and shoulder above the pack in your public speaking career. You've got oratory, charisma and also fascinating storytelling ability to wow your audience and make them keep listening to you without getting bored and tired. A career in public speaking as a sanguine, is certainly one of the best for you. You could get hired by individuals, companies, top brands and business organizations to speak in their shows, seminars and exhibitions. You could also be hired by political parties during political campaigns to woo supporters. Selling yourself or your own products through speaking to the public will also not be a huge task for you.

Customer Service Relationship:

No other temperament knows how to woo, attract, and relate with clients and customers in a way that'll make them keep coming back to patronize a business more than typical sanguines. Being a natural people-oriented personality, puts you ahead of others in this career. As a typical sanguine, attracting new customers, keeping existing ones and building a longtime relationship is one of your core strength, and you will derive fulfilment meeting, interacting and relating with different customers to make sure they're satisfied. There are various prospects and opportunities in this career. Because companies, brands, and business organizations are always looking to hire the best person that can attract new customers and clients to their business, and also build and maintain relationship with existing ones, in order to keep them coming back. Thus, as a typical sanguine, you're the best person that perfectly fits into this career because of your liveliness, happy-charisma and people-oriented qualities. You will definitely not find it difficult relating cordially with every client and customer.

Nursing:

Nursing is one of the best formal career that a predominant sanguine will definitely do very well in especially if your secondary temperament is phlegmatic. You will also feel very satisfied and fulfilled if you embark on this career path. This is because a nurse is expected to be caring, lively, compassionate and patient. The liveliness of a typical sanguine combined with the other qualities in congeniality with a phlegmatic as secondary temperament will obviously enable a predominant sanguine to be an exceptional nurse. Sanguines are naturally very lively, happy, hilarious and highly spirited individuals who uses these qualities and their natural warmth to lift the spirit and mood of anyone who is downtrodden. Many patients often responds very positively to a sanguine nurses' questions of "how are you today" Or "are you getting better" more than they will to any other temperament. This is because they know that the sanguine nurse has got the temperament that could give them courage and lift their spirits. This is why nursing is a very good career for predominant sanguines, and the excitement of meeting and interacting with new patients daily is the icing on the cake for them.

Politics is also another career that a predominant sanguine will find very interesting and attractive. For the sanguine is a people-oriented individual, who has got the capacity to mobilize and build bridges across different divides, thus rallying the support of everyone with his oratory, outspokenness, very high spirit. If his secondary temperament is choleric in substantial amount, it will enable him to be more assertive, disciplined, courageous, and influential. A blend or combination of sanguine and choleric temperament will no doubt make the Sanguine-choleric personality appear to be a very credible candidate that will be able to pool the crowd towards himself, and get them to entrust him with their votes. But whether they will eventually succeed in leadership or deliver on their mandate is a different kettle of fish all together. Conclusively, predominant sanguine have got the smartness, people-oriented, charismatic, and expressive qualities that will enable them to navigate their way through politics.

Evangelist:

In Christianity as a religion, there are various callings and ministries giving by God to man, to function in different roles for the advancement of His kingdom. While some are called to be apostles, prophets, pastors, others are called to function as teachers, evangelists, and some were given the gift of helping people Ephesians 4:11-16. It is our duty as human beings to discover the areas we will fit perfectly into, for which we will use to effortlessly and efficiently do the work of God when we decide to go on this path. Effectiveness in ministry and in doing God's work requires that we identify our areas of calling, courtesy of the natural strengths and abilities He had endowed us with, so we can function effectively in the advancement of His kingdom. For the predominant sanguine personality, who is a natural people-oriented person, selfless but charismatic enough to talk to anyone even if they are total strangers. This quality qualifies him to be an evangelist who is charismatic enough to bring new people to the Kingdom of God. No other temperament has the capacity to pull a lot of people to God using his liveliness, charisma, and talking ability like the predominantly Holy Spirit-filled sanguine person. Therefore, as a sanguine personality, you can allow God to make use of these natural qualities in you and turn you into a great evangelist that will be very effective in bringing souls to His kingdom.

As long as the job is about creativity in the entertainment sector, and interfacing with people, but devoid of too much attention-to-detail, critical and analytical thinking, and also routines that seldom give them the opportunity to interact with people, predominant sanguines are perfectly suited for it. Sanguines are one of the most versatile persons on earth. They know how to navigate their way through life, and also in getting what they want. They can succeed in any career, provided such career is one that's not boring and often brings them face to face with people, so they will be able to freely display their flamboyant and vivacious lifestyle. It's for this reason that I've listed the above major career fields that you will effortlessly excel in and reach the top. In chapter eight, we will consider in detail some of the best career fields in the entertainment, humanitarian, creative industry, and public sector for the different blends of the sanguine personality.

NATURAL VOCATIONAL STRENGTHS OF SANGUINE PERSONALITY BLENDS.

If you are conversant with the theory of temperament as conceptualized by the Ancient Greek physician Hippocrates, and evidently explained by successive authors. Or if you are a regular reader of my blog posts, you'd have been informed that no individual is born with just one type of temperament. We are all carriers of two or more blends and combinations of the temperaments, but usually in varying degrees and proportions, and one will of course predominate the others. This is basically what we refer to as blends of temperament or personality blends. Since temperament is our inherited traits as a result of the genes and chromosomes that were naturally transferred to us from our parents and even much more from our grandparents during our conception. Thus, the coming together of two people of different origins by marriage perhaps with different genotypical make up or design, with the intention of reproducing kids actually makes this a possibility and a reality. Now based on the particular parent that we have their genes and chromosomes transferred to us in excess, it clearly validates the idea of the dominant and recessive temperaments. Therefore, while the predominant temperament also known as our primary temperament, will usually be more visible, and will also have a more domineering influence on our traits and behavioral pattern. It's basically the same way the recessive temperaments, referred to as our secondary temperament, will be less visible, but will definitely have a considerable amount of influence on us.

> "Everyone is born with two or more temperaments, one predominant and the others recessive".

Having cleared the issue of temperament or personality blends, let us understand how temperament relates to vocation which we have discussed already in chapter one of this book. But in this chapter, we want to consider some of the major natural vocational strengths of the various blends of sanguine temperament, that will enable them to be very successful in certain jobs and careers. These are vocational strengths or qualities that the various combination or blends of the sanguine personality is born with, that will naturally aid each of them to succeed in certain careers and be efficient in doing their jobs. The sanguine personality blends, or any other blend for that matter is divided into three.

For the sanguine blends of temperament wherein sanguine predominates, the three blends are; Sanguine-choleric or Sanchol, Sanguine-melancholy, known as Sanmel, and Sanguine-phlegmatic, also referred to as Sanphleg. These three blends of the sanguine temperament, even though they have sanguine in common but they've got innate strengths and weaknesses that are different from each other. But we want to consider just their natural strengths that will help them succeed in certain vocations or jobs and careers that matched their vocational strengths and capabilities. But it is very instructive to know that there are three major career fields that the natural strengths of the predominant sanguine personality will allow him to effortlessly and overwhelmingly succeed in. They are mainly in the; Entertainment, Marketing and Sales, Creative, Public sectors, and in some humanitarian career fields. Thus, the different jobs and careers under these four major fields that each blend of sanguine temperament will fit in perfectly, will be largely dependent on the particular type of secondary temperament that the sanguine personality possessed. Having said that, let's now dive into considering the natural vocational strengths of various blends of the sanguine personality, starting with the Sanchol personality blend?

Natural Vocational Strengths Of Sanchol Personality Blends:

The Sanchol personality is obviously the strongest extrovert of the twelve blends of temperaments; for the two temperaments that combined to make up his personality are both of the extrovert category, wherein the predominant which is sanguine, is the most extroverted personality. He is easily the most active, expressive, and outgoing of sanguine personality blend. The major strengths of this personality are those that will enable him to be highly successful in outdoor activities, and rarely will he be hidden in the crowd. This personality knows how to navigate his way through with people or any situation, and get what he wants. He will care less about long time human interpersonal relationship even though he is people-oriented since sanguine is his primary temperament, unless it is for purpose of getting what he wants. The sanguine personality usually care more about things rather than being too much attached to someone. Initiating and building a relationship just to have his way with you, doing things his own way, and having you pander towards him after he might have successfully initiated the relationship and ignited your interest in him is not uncommon for the Sanchol personality blend. Let us consider some of his main strengths that will of course aid him to be effortlessly successful in certain jobs and careers that naturally aligned with his vocational capabilities.

Creative-Driving:

A Sanguine-choleric or Sanchol personality blend is a creative-driver; for the two basic temperaments that combined to form his personality are both creative and driving. While his predominant sanguine side is a natural creator, thus will be very creative in generating new ideas and concepts, his secondary choleric aspect will usually propel him to drive the idea to either become productive or be persuasive enough in selling it to those who can bring it into reality. This personality may not be much a detailed, analytical, or highly intelligent, but he sure knows how to navigate his way through with people and achieve what he wants from them. He is rather very smart and wise, than brilliant and intelligent. What he cannot get through the right and just way, he will get it through his smartness and assertiveness. He uses his smartness, assertiveness, and liveliness to talk you into believing and accepting his proposal. He is not so much passionate about people or maintaining a long-time relationship; for he is charismatic enough to make you do what he wants, and while his secondary choleric temperament also makes him self-sufficient enough to do most things for himself. His predominant sanguine aspect is smart and creative enough to figure out new ways of doing things or very uncommon things that will get your attention, pander towards him, and have you do he wants.

His vocational strengths usually tilts more towards things rather than directly towards people. Therefore, generating new concepts and ideas, suggestions or things that people will be very interested in, packaging and getting things done his own way, and also presenting something in a way that will catch the attention of everyone, and have them follow and become interested in what he proposes are no doubt the natural strengths that makes this personality blend effortlessly successful in some vocations, careers or jobs that these strengths and qualities are required. The best career fields that this vocational strength will be perfectly fit for are those in; Marketing and Sales, creative industry, and some careers in the entertainment sector.

Charismatic:

A Sanchol personality is also charismatic. For the two basic temperaments that make up his nature possess natural charisma. His basic sanguine temperament usually ignites his happy-charisma towards people, and make them easily pander to him. The charismatic nature of his secondary choleric side also enables him to motivate others to key into his vision and do what he wants. A Sanchol personality blend has got enough charisma to burn. He's rarely shy or scared of approaching or talking to anyone if he wants them to do something or maybe take a particular action. Consequently, it is usually not uncommon for these personalities to often have their way with people, and make others look up to them. I honestly believe that the Sanchol personalities are gifted with some natural social engineering skills they use to psychologically manipulate people into giving out sensitive information or doing what they want. No other temperament blend comes close to having the charisma of a typical Sanchol, and his ability to use psychology to subtly manipulate people into doing what he wants. Of course, this natural strength hitherto enables them to succeed in marketing and persuasion jobs and careers, and maybe some leadership duties.

Expressive/Assertive:

Although predominant sanguines are good talkers. They often talk more than anyone else, and highly expressive of themselves wherever they are. However, their words usually lacks corresponding actions. Thus, talking much more than they actually do is not uncustomary. Their actions are also usually more rather superficial than profound, lacking in depth and seriousness to make it effective. But when combined with the secondary choleric temperament in considerable amount, which is naturally more deliberate and assertive in speech, it makes the Sanchol personality blend an expressive as well as assertive personality. This consequently makes his words to be more potent, believable, and taken more seriously. Being expressive/assertive is one of the natural strengths of typical sanguine personality blends that makes them highly influential, and enables them to succeed in sales and marketing jobs, leadership and also in some public service careers.

Outspoken & Outgoing:

Among the twelve blends of temperament, there's no other blend that is so outspoken and outgoing like a Sanchol personality. He is rarely shy or afraid of speaking his mind, and saying it the way he feels. And no one can also be more outgoing than him. This is because the two basic temperaments that combined to form his personality are of the extrovert category, who are both naturally outspoken and outgoing. Consequently, this strength enables him to build and maximize his self-confidence, boldness and courage in addressing people, and standing before a crowd of people to speak boldly to them without being shy, or overwhelmed by any kind of stage fright. These personalities do not struggle to display these qualities, and make it easier to have an understanding of who they are, what they want, and how to relate with them.

Highly Sophisticated:

I have related with so many sanguines and cholerics, and have watched and observed them with keen interest the way they live their lives and do things. I discovered that these personalities seem to be somewhat ahead when it comes to the vicissitudes of life. I struggle to be very much adept about life as they are, as primarily a melancholy that I am, and perhaps be a little bit more adventurous. But I find it so difficult to be very skillful and adventurous about life as they are. Then, I later realized that some people are just naturally very adept about life and adventuresome, thus making them appear more sophisticated in life than others. While so many people are born with this traits, and it does not take them a long time to learn, become very skilled, and adapt so easily to their environment. Others usually tends to take quite sometime to learn and become very skilled in, or about the things of life.

Consequently, I discovered that majority of the people who are highly sophisticated because of their natural quest for adventures and adeptness about life, belong to people of the extrovert category, such as sanguine and choleric. For the sanguine, because of his smart, social, outgoing, plus his innate adventurous qualities makes him appear more sophisticated. While the innate wise and discerning nature of a typical choleric is the springboard of his sophistication. So when these two basic temperaments are blended together, it obviously makes the Sanchol a highly sophisticated personality, who is easily the first to become aware of latest trends and happenings in the world, especially in technology and the entertainment sector. This usually enables them to stay ahead of the phlegmatics and melancholies in terms of latest trends in fashion, business, technology, and human relations.

Business Oriented:

The people-oriented, salesmanship, and marketing nature of the typical sanguine personality, combined with the productive and influential nature of a predominant Choleric, plus his love for independence, absolutely makes Sanchols very business minded and oriented personalities. Apart from their Sanmel and perhaps Sanphleg counterparts to an extent who comes close, no other temperament blend type usually succeeds in business more than a Sanchol personality blends. For they know how to use their natural charisma, high influence, sophistication, practicality, word of mouth and oratory to sell their products. They've got more customers and clients who often patronizes their business . These blends no know how to package very substandard or bad product, market it with their word of mouth, and make sales, which others may not be able to do. They have what it takes to even sell crutches to someone who is not crippled, only for them to get home and realize that they do not need it, and should not have bought it. But they were probably overwhelmed or ravaged by the Sanchol's salesmanship ability to convince him to buy it. It's basically for this reason that careers in business is also where their strength lies.

Creative/Productive:

Even though predominant sanguines are rarely productive persons, but if they have choleric as their secondary temperament in considerable amount, it will definitely make a sanchol personality blend creative as well as a productive personality especially when it comes to physical products, deliverables, and services. This personality will not only be creative in his imagination and thoughts, but he also has the ability to make his imaginations come alive. For the practicality, dexterity, and of course productivity of his choleric side will enable him bring his creative imagination to reality. It's basically for this reason that a typical Sanchol is usually very curious, he's rarely afraid of trying out some of his new ideas, skills, and adventures. This strength enables him to be more practical and real than theoretical and ethereal. His sanguine aspect can imagine or visualize something, while his secondary choleric side will give him the ability to bring it to reality. It is of course the reason why some of them are very good in creative arts, such as drawing, sculpture, painting and other products that are entertaining. The three blends of the sanguine personality possess this strength, but usually display it in different career fields.

Both sanguine and choleric personalities are rarely theoretical people by nature. They are rather more practical, and often thrives better in real than ideal situations. The adventurous nature of the sanguine blended with the pragmatism and love for practicality of the choleric makes the Sanchol personality blend a highly technical person who is naturally skilled in a practical ways in attending to technically demanding tasks. It is for this reason that he often out-performs his Sanmel and Sanphleg counterparts in technical careers or jobs.

Let us now consider some of the natural vocational strengths of the Sanmel blends.

Natural Vocational Strengths Of Sanmel Personality Blends:

The Sanmel personality blends are better off described as ambiverts just like their Sanphleg counterparts. For unlike Sanchols who are pure extroverts, since the two basic temperaments which combined to make their blend are both of the extrovert stock. But for a Sanmel, this personality has got both extrovert and introvert qualities combined. Wherein his predominant sanguine aspect will make him to more often behave like an extrovert , and at other times, he will be influenced by his melancholy side to make him act more like an introvert. Nevertheless, these personality will usually be more often than not influenced by the sanguine side, since it's predominant, and by some percentages higher than his secondary melancholy side. In this blend, some of the excesses and weaknesses of the sanguine is usually curtailed and made less impactful by his secondary melancholy temperament because both sanguine and melancholy have almost equal impact on the behavioral pattern of someone especially if they're in the ratio of 55:45 or 60:40, both of them will have almost the same amount of influence even though sanguine predominates. For instance, the sanguine who's highly undisciplined, very impulsive, and garrulous will be a bit more disciplined, strategic, and organized in his speech. Sanmel personality blends are also people-oriented. They are one of the most friendly, hospitable, and amiable persons to relate with, and have as companions. For they're usually very concerned about the wellbeing and comfortability of others. These blends are easily the most emotional of the twelve blends of temperaments.

For both sanguine and melancholy are the two most emotional of the four basic type of temperaments. Thus, when combined together, they make the Sanmel personality a highly emotional individual. He may get so emotional over little act of kindness just like his opposite Melsan counterpart, and it will lift him to heights of great ecstasy. He could also become very emotional over a very trivia matter, or just at the slightest provocation that could make him explode in anger. However, they are good-natured human beings who easily feels the pains of others and tries to help them get out of it. Nevertheless, they are not as much open to, and interested in people as the Sanphlegs are. For their melancholy aspect that enjoys privacy tries to moderate their interest in others, and how frequently they relate with them. Vocationally, the strengths of Sanmel personality blends tilts more often towards doing things, or coming up with innovations and ideas that tends to make others feel happy, satisfied, comfortable, and ameliorate the effect of whatever pain they may be going through. It tilts more towards improving the quality of life of people.

Let us consider some of the natural strengths that often enables them to be overwhelmingly successful in certain jobs and careers that matched their vocational strengths.

Creative Thinking:

Just like the melancholy personality blends who are unarguably the most creative thinkers of all the blends, Sanmel blends are also the most creative thinkers of the sanguine blends of temperament. For the natural creativity of a sanguine combined with the intelligence and analytical ability of the melancholy to make a Sanmel blend a highly creative thinking person. These blends possess the innate ability to quickly innovate new ideas, or creatively think out new solutions to problems. Sometimes, the creative thinking ability of this personality blend comes to the fore during their quiet and calm moments when alone in a serene environment. It is basically for this reason that they're very good fiction book writers; for the creativity in fascinating storytelling of their sanguine side is combined with the natural analytical skills and perfectionism of their melancholy aspect to enable them write very good fiction books. Similarly, the passion for problem-solving of melancholy propels and triggers the creative thinking ability of the Sanmel blend personality to figure out how to solve problems. These strength sure enables them to be successful in most careers in entertainment industry, the creative industry, humanitarian careers, and in any vocation where creative and innovative thinking ability is needed.

Smart/Intelligent:

The Sanmel blend is a smart as well as an intelligent personality; but he will usually display smartness than intelligence since his predominant sanguine side influences him to be rather smart than intelligent. But if his secondary melancholy side is in high or substantial amount, then, he'll equally be influenced by both temperaments. This strength ultimately enables him to be very strategic in his interpersonal relationship with others, and also efficient in what he does, and how he usually go about getting people to become passionate about what he is got to offer. For this blend, the smartness of the sanguine is blended with the intelligence of the melancholy to enable the Sanmel personality blend easily navigate through life, and be tremendously successful in so many jobs and careers that matched this vocational strength. Some jobs and careers in marketing, advertising, entertainment, and business are perfect fit for him.

Expressive/Analytical:

The Sanmel personality blend is detailed and analytical because of the melancholy aspect of him. He's got so much admirable qualities that often endears him to people, and makes relating with him seamless and worthwhile. However, having a secondary melancholy temperament that allows him keep to himself and be more often than not a private person, consequently conceal his natural personable qualities. But a natural combination of the sanguine temperament who is outgoing and expressive, allows all his fine qualities to become very visible and appreciated by everyone that encounters him. When the very expressive nature of the sanguine is blended with the analytical ability of the melancholy, it makes Sanmel personalities very persuasive, analytical, and comprehensibly clear speakers who seldom make you feel bored listening to them. You could spend hours granting him audience without getting bored because he usually tends to analyze very complex and intricate facts using very real and relatable illustrations to make you understand. It is for this reason that some careers in public, entertainment, and also in religious sectors are very good for him.

Creative-Efficient:

Sanmel personalities are not just creatives, but they are also efficient in what they do. The productivity and perfectionism of their melancholy side naturally blends with the creativity of the sanguine to make Sanmel blends both creative and efficient persons. This strength among others enables them to be result oriented by conceptualizing marketable ideas that are practicable in nature. It's for this reason that they're very efficient in any type of creative art works that requires high efficiency. Careers in the creative and entertainment industry are no doubt where this natural strength can be effectively deployed.

Compassionate/Sacrificing:

As stated earlier, Sanmel personalities are the most emotional of the twelve blends of temperaments. They can't stand watching a tragic movie, or beholding a gory site, or seeing some inhumane treatment melted out to a fellow human being without shedding tears and crying profusely. The unfortunate experiences of others easily emotes a melancholic feeling in them that could make them burst into tears. There's no other temperament that quickly expresses sympathy or compassion towards the unpleasant experiences of others more than a predominant sanguine. However, since he's not a profound person who is deep in his thought and actions, it could only end up in just commiserating with you without an extra effort to seeing how he can get you out of that unfortunate situation. But when this natural act of compassion and sympathy is combined with the innate self-sacrificing qualities of a melancholy who is much more profound and real in his actions and thoughts, it clearly makes the Sanmel personality blend the go-to person whenever you're in a predicament. Even though his predominant sanguine side may attempt to make him unwilling to long-suffer with you, but his melancholy side in considerable amount has got the patience to stick with you until everything is fine. It's basically for this reason that the Sanmel personalities among the blends of sanguine temperament do exceptionally well in any humanitarian career because they've got the natural strengths that helps them to be effortlessly successful in this field.

Enterprising:

Apart from the Sanchol blends who comes distant close, Sanmel blends possessed the most enterprising skill and ability, which enables them to easily decipher some new business ventures and opportunities. The natural creativity of the sanguine when combined with the natural enterprising, forward thinking, and analytical ability of the melancholy, it obviously makes Sanmel personalities highly enterprising. They've got the foresight, imaginative ability, plus the natural instinct of the melancholy to be able to see some business opportunities in certain things that appears too common, which others might not see. Asides the Melsans, and Melchols to an extent, no other blend have innovated more new business idea or figured out some business opportunities that is non-existent in a particular place but has high potential of profitability more than the Sanmel personality blend. Like I said earlier, the natural creativity of the sanguine, together with the analytical, high intelligence, and also foresightedness of the melancholy in Sanmel, undoubtedly makes the Sanmel personality blend highly enterprising. It is basically for this reason that making a business off entertainment, and discovering business opportunities in certain career fields is no doubt areas they usually do exceptionally well.

Responsive:

Responsiveness is definitely one admirable natural strength you can't take away from Sanmel personality blends. While Sanchol blends may be too busy with some external activities therefore, may not always be there to attend to critical issues affecting others or even those under their care, and Sanphleg blends will usually hesitate and dilly-dally in responding quickly to the pain points of others or may be clueless about what to do. The Sanmel personality blends are naturally empowered, and are usually motivated to react and respond quickly and positively to the pain points of others, and see how they can rescue or bring succor to them. For the natural enthusiasm of the sanguine, and his compassion towards people combined with the hospitality, conscientiousness, and self-sacrificing ability of a melancholy, unarguably makes Sanmel personality blend the most responsive of the sanguine blends, who is usually passionate about the comfort and well-being of everyone. It's for this reason that they make very good and responsive leaders, and one of the best human managers.

Finally, let us consider some major natural strengths of Sanphleg personality blends which enables them to be successful in certain career fields that ranks even with these strengths.

Of the three sanguine temperament blends, the Sanphleg personality blends seems to be the most misunderstood in terms of their traits and behavioral patterns. Sometimes, their lifestyle and dispositions is usually misconstrued with those of their Sanmel counterparts since they are also regarded as ambiverts. This misrepresentation of both personality blends are nonetheless quite understandable, because melancholy and phlegmatic personalities are so closely related in their outward dispositions and how they approach issues. But make no mistake about it, these two personalities though of the same introvert category, are so markedly different from each other in their traits and genotypical build up. It is far more realistically correct to compare and draw analogies between a predominant sanguine and phlegmatic personalities even though they're not of the same category. But when it comes to their natural desires and some things that they usually pander towards, both of them shares similarities. For instance, these two personalities are so much passionate about people, and they are always interested in others. They love being with, and around people but while a sanguine is often very loud and expressive about his desire for others, and he is more often than not the first person to make the move of initiating a conversation that could lead to a relationship with someone. The phlegmatic personality who also enjoys the company of people like the sanguine, but he is usually very reserved, unexpressive or quiet about it, but often expects or relish others to always show interest in him first and come to him.

Additionally, predominant sanguine and phlegmatic are the two temperaments that love to be noticed, recognize or given attention. But while a sanguine will make use of his flamboyance, exuberance and vivacious lifestyle to get everyone to notice him. A typical phlegmatic usually believes that his natural quiet, calm and collected, organized, and humble disposition should make everyone pander to him. So, these two temperaments are passionate about people, and it excites them when they are eulogized and complimented by people, in fact, human beings are their main source of strength. But how they usually go about achieving their desires is basically what makes the difference between them. From this fact that has been clearly stated, it can be inferred that the typical Sanphleg personality blend will be highly passionate about people, interacting and relating very closely with others is for sure their utmost source of excitement. Being alone, and without the company of people in an ambience of fun and camaraderie will be very boring for them. Consequently, most of their vocational strengths will naturally tilts towards human beings, jobs or careers that often expose them to people, or make people pander towards them are usually where these strengths can be effectively deployed. And it is of course where they will derive their source of fulfilment and satisfaction in life. Let us quickly consider some of these strengths that will enable them to overwhelmingly succeed in Jobs or careers matched these natural strengths. It is instructive to know that whatever career or job a Sanphleg will be efficient in, such jobs must be human being related, or must be something that people will compliment and eulogize him for his efficiency and efforts.

Creative Arts & Crafts:

Creative arts and crafts is easily an aspect of entertainment that Sanphleg blends will usually deploy their natural creativity, and be productive. The natural creativity of the sanguine combined with the efficiency and aptitude of the phlegmatic usually enables a Sanphleg personality to produce so many creative art works and crafts that everyone admires their ingenuity and creativity. So, these personalities are good in various art works that expresses emotions or feelings, and visions. For instance, some of the arts works they are very good and efficient in, are; drawing, calligraphy, literature, print making, theatre, music, dance, choreography, performing arts etc. For craft; paper making, needle work, fashion design, leather works, watch and phone repair, fiber and textile, houseware, flower crafts, glass making, weaving, etc. are some of the crafts that typical Sanphleg personalities are naturally empowered to be productive in, if only they're intentional about deploying their innate strength in these field.

Smart & Clever:

Sanphleg personality blends combines the natural smartness of the sanguine, plus the cleverness or craftiness of the phlegmatic, thus enabling them to have their way, and get what they want from people easily. Just as the Sanchol makes use of his smartness/wisdom, plus charisma to outsmart others, or make people do what he wants, while the Sanmel will use his natural smartness/intelligence to navigate his way through with people. The Sanphleg blend is known for using his smartness and cleverness to either outsmart you, or get you to pander towards what he wants if you are easily ravaged by his warmth and congeniality. It's basically for this reason that if perhaps he is a retailer or business person, he knows how to make use of his natural smart and clever lifestyle to woo potential customers and clients to patronize his business and sell his products. He may also make use of these qualities to get favor from anyone, or use them to outwit his competitors or very naïve and unsuspecting people.

People-oriented:

Of the twelve blends of temperaments, no blend comes close to the people-oriented and congenial qualities of the Sanphleg personality blends. This is because the two temperaments that combined to make up their nature are both people-oriented, and have got almost similar outward admirable qualities that gets people attracted to them. Both sanguines and phlegmatics naturally possess congenial qualities which usually enables their people-oriented lifestyle. It is just that a sanguine is expressive about his, while a phlegmatic is usually reserved. Notwithstanding, when these two temperaments are blended in a person it makes him highly people-oriented, and such individual will often display his affection for people and will always relish spending time with them. These personalities will of course be very enthusiastic about people, and always want to create a deeper, peaceful, and cordial relationship with everyone around them. Consequently, succeeding in sales and marketing jobs, or some humanitarian careers will rarely be a difficult task for them.

Light-hearted:

Light-heartedness, or always been happy and cheerful is one major natural strength you can't deny about Sanphleg personality blends. No other temperament blend can be more light-hearted than the Sanphleg personalities. For the natural combination of easygoing, fun loving, overindulgence of the sanguine, with love for camaraderie in an ambience of enjoyment, peaceful, and non-abrasive lifestyle of the phlegmatic are sufficient to make a Sanphleg personality blend the most light-hearted of the twelve blends. He rarely gets upset, very amusing, and showing very little to no seriousness in almost everything he does. No one can be more cheerful and happy than a Sanphleg blend. He has the highest boiling point and lowest volatility that he almost never boil, or become volatile. As a result, he doesn't find relationship with others difficult. In fact, he is friend to everyone around, and so many people gets easily attracted to him because of these qualities. Even those who perhaps were initially averse to his talkative and unserious lifestyle, tends to get used to it, and take him for who he is. Some careers and jobs in public service where they can meet and interact with people, marketing, and entertainment sectors are basically where he can deploy this natural strength.

Helping People:

The enthusiasm of a sanguine personality towards people, plus his compassionate nature is naturally blended with the nice and kindheartedness of the phlegmatic to make the Sanphleg personality blend one of the most hospitable, and helpers of people if and when they do decide to help. Helping people is these personalities lifestyle, and their regular business. They usually derive excitement and satisfaction bringing succor to people. It's basically for this reason that they usually do very well in humanitarian and social welfare jobs and careers.

Humorous:

Even though they're the least extroverted of the sanguine temperament blends who are often regulated by circumstances and their environment. Sanphlegs are the most humorous of sanguine personality blends; for the natural congenial qualities of both temperaments, plus the liveliness and fun loving nature of typical sanguine personality makes the Sanphleg a very humorous and hilarious person. They are extremely happy and easily excited people, who their carefree nature and good humor makes them that lighthearted entertainer that is always sought after by others. These personalities enjoys people a lot and they are also very passionate about others enjoying them. Therefore, doing things to make others happy and excited by being hilarious and comical in their conversation and friendly disposition is not uncommon for them. Some careers in the entertainment and humanitarian fields are of course best areas this strength can be utilized.

Adaptability:

Apart from a Sanchol personality blend who comes close, no other temperament adapts seamlessly, to a new environment more than a Sanphleg personality blend. For the natural liveliness and outgoing lifestyle of a typical sanguine, and his charisma, when blended with the calm, peaceful, and non-abrasive qualities of a phlegmatic, are some of the basic features that enables a Sanphleg personality blend to easily adapt to a new environment and relate quite well with everyone around. While other blends are still trying to settle in, and get use to the way of life of people within the environment, which often takes them sometime, a Sanphleg personality has no difficulty with that, since he is naturally a people's person. It is for this reason that some marketing and entertainment field jobs and careers are usually the best for his personality. They also do very well in an ambassadorial and missionary works because of this quality.

In conclusion, sanguine personalities are the most extroverted and people-oriented of the four basic temperament types. Thus, the blends of this personality will no doubt also be the most extroverted of the twelve blends of temperament. But the difference in their degree of extroversion will largely depend on the secondary temperament. As these differences are real, and makes each of them unique and distinct in their own way, so also their natural strengths which enables them to effortlessly thrive in some jobs and careers are very real. And this is basically what we refer to as the vocational strengths or capabilities of the personality or temperament blends.

CHAPTER SEVEN

BEST CAREERS FOR SANGUINE PERSONALITY BLENDS.

> "Becoming the best in a broad niche requires micro-niching, to become the best in a broad career field you've got to specialize in a sub-career".

We have clearly stated it creativity, liveliness, charisma, outgoing, and predominant sanguine that the natural people-oriented, happy-expressive qualities of a personality makes him perfectly fit for careers in the creative industry, marketing and sales, entertainment industry, some humanitarian jobs, and any other job that allows him the opportunity to freely express himself, without requiring too much attention-to-detail, meticulousness, critical and analytical thinking, and routines that seldom allows him the freedom to interface with people. However, the various sub-careers in these sectors or industries that the predominant sanguine will be perfectly fit for, and be very exceptional in the discharge of his job will certainly depend on the secondary temperament of the sanguine personality. For instance, even though sanguine is predominant in a Sanchol blend, but a Sanchol will find it difficult to do well in humanitarian careers or jobs ahead of a Sanmel or Sanphleg, or be better than a Sanmel in major sectors of the creative industry. This is basically because the natural strengths of the choleric temperament in a Sanchol is not well suited for those fields. However, there's no doubt that there are other areas in those industry that a typical Sanchol will be head and shoulder above both a Sanmel and Sanphleg personality blends, because his secondary temperament possess strengths and qualities that's required to succeed in them that those two blends are destitute of. Therefore, our secondary temperament is as important as our primary or predominant, because it also possess some natural strengths and capabilities that helps us to be more specialized in different career fields or be exceptional in some fields that are generally relevant to our temperament blends. Consequently in this chapter, we want to consider various sub-careers in those major career fields or industries earlier stated, that ranked even with the sanguine personality blends. These lists of sub-careers will definitely be more about the secondary temperament strengths of the sanguine personality blends. I will suggest that you make more research about these career fields, and know the trainings or courses required to sharpen your natural vocational skills in them, in order to seamlessly advance in them.

BEST JOBS AND CAREERS FOR SANCHOL PERSONALITIES:

Asides all of the basic natural strengths or qualities of the predominant sanguine which is common in all the blends wherein sanguine predominates, the major strengths that will keep a Sanchol personality blend head and shoulder above his Sanmel and Sanphleg counterparts in these jobs or career fields are; the assertive, charismatic, and self-sufficiency of the secondary choleric, plus the sophistication and natural technical know-how of both the sanguine and choleric, which are not common in the other two blends.

There are various aspects of, or fields in the entertainment industry which a Sanchol personality blend will be best suited for, and be ahead of Sanphleg and Sanmel especially if they have to work alone or be independent. And as long as they do not require too much attention-to-detail, analysis, and long range planning, but are very practical in nature, requiring energy and physical productivity. Let us consider some of these careers and see if they rank even with your personality as a Sanchol personality blend.

Sports athletes:

Even though any of sanguine blend or any of temperament blends for that may choose to go into sports, I honestly believe that the Sanchol, and their opposite blend, Cholsan are better for this career. For Sports is an outdoor activity that requires less brain work, but the willingness to express and showcase your natural skills and ability to others. It is an aspect of entertainment that a typical Sanchol will be efficient in. For the natural energy and strong determination of the choleric to win in any competition, combined with the smartness of the sanguine will doubtlessly enable the Sanchol become a successful sports person or athlete. But he will do better in individual sporting events which does not require working with a team to succeed. He could succeed in football, basketball, or any other team sport, but his poor human interpersonal relationship will often tend to put a clog in the wheel of his progress in competitions where other team members have to bring their best for the team to succeed.

Cinematography:

A Sanmel may come close to a Sanchol in this career, because of the perfectionism of the secondary melancholy temperament. But the high sophistication and technical ability of a Sanchol will definitely put him above his Sanmel counterpart in this career path. This is because the technical aspects of images, such as the lighting and lens choices requires the technical capability of the Sanchol personality blend.

Hair and Fashion Stylist:

The creativity of the sanguine combined with the self-sufficiency, sophistication, skillfulness of the choleric, and the desire to be different from others, or do things differently from what others have done or are doing, may trigger a typical Sanchol personality to create his own Hair and Fashion style which others may want to later copy or adopt.

Entertainment law- Cyber lawyer:

This is an aspect of the law profession in the entertainment industry that a Sanchol personality blend is pre-qualified to venture into. For his natural technical ability, adeptness in the use of technology, and vastness in the entertainment sector, consequently makes him interested in knowing what his rights are, and also the laws guiding the entertainment industry, so he can stoutly defend his client with his assertiveness. No one is more adept in cyber laws, and enjoys the profession more than a typical Sanchol or their Cholsan counterparts because of their natural sophistication, legal consciousness, and courage.

Production Coordinator:

The capacity to coordinate all aspects of an entertainment program undoubtedly requires the outspokenness of both sanguine and choleric, plus the productivity, charismatic, and leadership ability of the choleric to ensure that all relevant departments do their job, for quality entertainment package. This is also a testament of his natural leadership capability.

Event Production Freelancer:

Sanchols are natural entertainment event producers who knows how to produce or create scenes of events. Consequently, the innate self-sufficiency and independence of the choleric usually enables them to become independent event producers that could be hired by someone, or sought after in the entertainment industry.

Videography:

Just like cinematography, the process of capturing video in a digital way, or capturing moving images in electronic media certainly requires the high sophistication and technical know-how of the choleric, but with little perfectionism of the melancholy in order to produce a high quality video that will be very interesting to watch.

Talent and Project Publicist:

Even though any of the Sanguine personality blend may be able to succeed in this career field, but I honestly believe that the charismatic, assertive, and social engineering skills and qualities of the Sanchol will enable him outperform his Sanmel and Sanphleg counterparts in this career. For the ability to effectively market, publicize, and promote a talent or project and get the buy-in and support of the public towards it, sure requires the aforementioned strengths of the Sanchol blends.

Artist Management:

This involves the publicization, marketing, and management of an upcoming artist until he or she becomes a brand. The edge a Sanchol personality has over the other blends in this career are his; charisma, sophistication, and business acumen. The strengths will definitely suffice to enable him to effectively package, market, and sell an upcoming artist to the world until he becomes a brand. However, he will need to possess some managerial skills in human management and relationship in order to maintain a long-time relationship with his client.

Film Actor:

A Sanchol could also do well in film acting, but his role should be clearly defined to him, it should be practical enough and full of actions. He must also be given time to practice and prepare himself for the role before coming on-set, because he does not have the amount of creativity, intelligence, and intuition of his Sanmel counterpart to quickly understand and assimilate his role within a short notice, and so real on stage like his Melsan opposite. However, a Sanchol has got the action, practicality, sophistication, to perform well in a movie role that doesn't require too much attention-to-details, analysis, or perfection.

Let's consider some fields in the humanitarian sector that a Sanchol personality will be suitable for.

Even though they are not natural humanitarians, but careers in the humanitarian sector are numerous, it is a very comprehensive sector, requiring a holistic approach in order to achieve some tremendous result. Therefore, some of the humanitarian careers that a typical Sanchol personality will be efficient in, are those that indirectly impacts positively on the lives of the people in need of these humanitarian services. Their pragmatism, coordination ability, outgoing and outspokenness, plus their productivity and high work rate will enable them to efficiently discharge their responsibility in these humanitarian fields.

. Humanitarian field coordinator.

The ability to manage all the humanitarian base teams in a humanitarian operation, and ensuring that each department in the base of operation is actually implementing the project or program plan, certainly requires the coordinating, hardworking, charismatic, and bargaining ability of the Sanchol personality. If given this task, he is outgoing, highly spirited, and charismatic enough to source and solicit support for humanitarian aids for those who may be displaced by war or natural disaster.

. Logistician:

Manages procurement, shipments, storage and transportation of humanitarian aids, and also ensures adequate supply of aids. His charismatic, outgoing and coordinating ability plus practical productivity and result-orientedness will enable him to succeed in this job, whether in the humanitarian or any other sector.

. Shelter coordinator:

Ensures the provision of temporary or long-term shelter for the people in need who have been displaced by either natural disaster or conflict. For as long as it has to do with construction and physical productivity, he will be efficient in it. Next to him in this job description are the Choleric blend of temperament.

.Program manager & Coordinator.

The ability to manage and coordinate various aspects and projects of the humanitarian operation in an operational base and ensuring that the program is carried out and completed as quickly as possible also requires the coordinating, hardworking, and charismatic abilities of the Sanchol personality.

. Camp coordinator.

Coordinating the camp or the operational base of the humanitarian program, and making sure that it is conducive and comfortable for the displaced to live in, requires the coordinating and leadership skills of the Sanchol personality in being able to assign different roles to those involved in the humanitarian operation.

. Protection Specialist:

The displaced persons in the humanitarian camps are usually very vulnerable to external attacks, therefore they need protection while they are undergoing recuperation. Apart from a Cholsan in the choleric blend who is bold, fearless and smart, or a Cholmel and their opposite Melchol who also naturally possess the fearlessness of the choleric and self-sacrificing ability of the melancholy, a Sanchol blend is one personality in the sanguine blend that is taunted to function better in this role, because of his energy, smartness, and fearlessness.

These are some of the careers in the humanitarian sector that a typical Sanchol personality blend will be very efficient in, when given the role and responsibility, even though he is rarely humanitarian in nature. The above listed natural qualities and capabilities will enable him to effectively and efficiently discharge his duties in these sector.

Let us consider some careers and jobs in the public sector that ranks even with a typical Sanchol personality natural strengths, where of course, he will be effortlessly successful both in acquiring a formal education or training and also practicing it in the field. It is instructive to know that the best careers or jobs for our personality are not only those we choose to study in college and maybe graduate with a degree in them. But they are those we can as well be efficient and innovative in on the field, when called upon to practice it or given the on field task. Here are some courses that a typical Sanchol personality will not only find unlaborious studying in college and graduating with a degree, but he will also display skill and competence practicing them in the field. As a rule, Sanchol personalities are usually attracted to art-related, and some social science courses rather than science based ones, since they are more practical nature than theoretical, rarely detail-oriented and analytical personalities, plus their averseness to any endeavor that will make them, overthink and overstress their brains. List of art courses they will be perfectly suitable for, are;

. **Law/Legal Advocates:**
. **Political science/Politician**
. **Marketing**
. **Mass communication.**
. **Applied arts.**
. **Archaeology.**
. **Sociology.**
. **Business Administration.**
. **History and diplomatic studies.**
. **Construction/Civil Engineering.**
. **Computer Engineering.**

BEST JOBS AND CAREERS FOR SANMEL PERSONALITIES:

Sanmels are the most gifted and talented of the sanguine personality blends. For apart from the natural creativity and happy charisma of the sanguine which is common to all blends of the sanguine. The melancholy side of the Sanmel blend possess high IQ, analytical and enterprising ability, self-sacrificing and responsive qualities, plus hounds for details and perfectionism which enables them excel exceedingly in almost any course they decide to go into, or jobs and careers that ranks even with these strengths. Any job that requires reasoning, analysis, self-sacrifice, responsiveness, making others feel better, and a perfection is very suitable for the Sanmel personality. However, because sanguine is predominant in him, all of the personable and admirable qualities of the melancholy may fully come to the fore. Therefore, it is in the melancholy personality blends wherein melancholy is predominant, that most of these qualities will fully accentuated. Having said that, let us consider some of the best jobs and careers that a typical Sanmel blend will be best suited for, both in theory and in practice.

When it comes to the humanitarian sector, Sanmels and their opposite Melsan blends are most naturally equipped to function optimally in this field. For the natural hospitable, accommodating, self-sacrificing, and conscientious qualities of the melancholy is combined with the people-oriented, compassionate, and tender-heartedness of the sanguine to make them exceptional in this field. Among the sanguine blend, next to Sanmel in the humanitarian field job is their Sanphleg counterpart because of their natural helping ability, but the level of their self-sacrifice and passion for the wellbeing of others to that of a Sanmel is incomparable. Consequently, a Sanmel personality blend can thrive in any aspect of the humanitarian job, including those earlier mentioned that are peculiar to Sanchols. But while a Sanchol will do well in those areas that indirectly impacts positively on the people such as; logistics, coordinating the humanitarian teams, and overseeing all programs and projects that will be required for the success of the humanitarian operation, a Sanmel takes on, and plays a deeper role in such areas that directly impacts positively on the life and livelihoods of the people. So, let us list some of these roles that a Sanmel will be perfectly suitable for;

. Emergency Response Personnel,

. Grant manager,

. Water and Sanitation engineer,

. Nutritionist,

. Medical coordinator,

. Foreign Aid Officer,

.Food security and livelihood coordinator,

. Legal Aid Officer/advocate,

. Monitoring and evaluation manager,

. Education manager,

Best humanitarian careers and Professions for Sanmel blend personalities:

. **Medical doctor/Physician:**

If his predominant sanguine temperament will allow him to discipline himself and go through the rigors of the medical school, or if the blend ratio between his primary sanguine and secondary melancholy is even, 50:50 or 55:45 percent ratio, wherein his secondary melancholy side is as influential on him as his primary temperament. A Sanmel personality will be able to undergo rigorous process of medical training because of his brilliance and intelligence, analytical ability, perfectionism, and practicality. Beyond this, the Sanmel medical doctor will also be very efficient in the discharge of his duty. He will be very passionate about upholding medical ethics of saving lives, because of his compassionate heart, conscientiousness, self-sacrificing qualities of his secondary melancholy side. He will usually induce quick recovery in his patients, because of his optimism, good temper, a heart full of compassion towards his fellow human, and a desire for the well-being of others.

. Nurse/Nursing Science,

. Physiotherapist,

. Dentists,

. Pediatrician,

. Gynecologist,

. Midwifery.

In these careers or professions, the natural compassion and enthusiasm of the sanguine towards others, combined with the conscientious, self-sacrificing, hospitable qualities and perfectionism of the melancholy will enable a Sanmel personality to effortlessly succeed in them, and discharge their duties with high efficiency.

Best Jobs In The Entertainment Sector For Sanmels:

I will highlight some of the most lucrative jobs in the entertainment industry that perfectly fits a typical Sanmel, which he can actually engage in, and earn a living for himself. We are not going into details about these jobs. I am making these recommendations based on your natural strengths, qualities, and potentials you possessed as a Sanmel that will enable you to effortlessly succeed in this jobs and be exceptional in them. It's basically your duty to make more research about them, and the trainings you are required to undergo in order to sharpen your innate skills in them. Let us consider some of the best jobs or work in the entertainment industry that a typical Sanmel will be very well suited for, and the natural strengths that will enable him outperform his counterparts in this field.

. Athletic/Sports Director,

. Sports Event planner,

. Sports Analyst,

. On-stage acting,

. Creative writing,

. Makeup artist,

. Event planning & decoration,

. Film production,

. Production designer,

. Creative producer,

. Game Analyst,

. Tour management,

. Publicity management,

. Entertainment management,

. Commercial gallery art management,

. Creative arts.

The natural creativity, happy-charisma, and people-centric qualities of the sanguine, blended with the high IQ, efficiency, enterprising, management, strategic and analytical thinking ability of the melancholy will certainly enable a Sanmel personality effortlessly succeed in these entertainment jobs, and his realisms and emotions will usually be prominent in his art works or products.

Some major courses or fields of study a Sanmel student will likely do very well in, in college, get a degree in them and also possess the natural strengths that will enable him to display skills and competence in on-field practice. Best of the secondary melancholy blend in Sanmel, a Sanmel personality will be able to also do well in some science related courses, asides art and social science disciplined where majority of his strength lies. Some examples of courses a Sanmel students can study in college that matched his natural strengths includes;

. Public, Civil, and international law & relations,

. Advertising and Marketing,

. Psychology,

. Sociology,

. Film and media arts,

. Effective communication studies,

. Archeology,

. Anthropology,

. International relations,

. Mass communication,

. Theatre arts,

. Political science,

. Public administration,

. Linguistics,

. Literature and literary studies,

. Music,

. Fine and applied arts,

. Education/Teaching,

. Guidance and counseling,

. Nursing and nursing science.

One major science subject a predominant sanguine finds interesting in high school or college is biology. His brain is wired to quickly understand and assimilate activities within his environment or something he can relate to in real life, such as the study of plants and animals. Therefore, fields or courses that are partly biologically base are good for him. **Microbiology** is one field he will certainly do well in. Similarly, Because of his secondary melancholy temperament that is usually very theoretical, analytical, and have got some mathematical capability, it will also enable a Sanmel to do very well in **biochemistry** and **biophysics**. And finally, **biotechnology** is also another field he will not find difficult to graduate with a degree in, and also practice as a biotechnologist.

Conclusively, any course or discipline that has to do with being creative, analytical reasoning, effective communication, public relations, and making use of his smartness and intelligence is best for a typical Sanmel personality.

Other jobs a Sanmel personalities can take on full or part-time are;

. Public speaking,
. Content creation,
. Copywriting,
. Public relations,
. News and sports Analyst,
. Painting,
. Sculpture,
. Visual arts,
. Fine and applied arts,
. Music,
. Drawing,
. Photography,
. Performance art,
. Architecture,
. Printmaking,
. Decorative art,
. Fiction book writing.

Any other form of art or job that requires creative thinking, analytical reasoning, and perfectionism are best suitable for a Sanmel personality. Sanmel personalities finds their true meaning in life, fulfilment and satisfaction when they are able to create or do something that adds value to life, and impacts positively on the lives of others.

BEST JOBS AND CAREERS FOR SANPHLEG PERSONALITIES:

Sanphleg personalities are the most people-oriented of the sanguine blend. They are the least serious or most complacent of the sanguine blend, consequently trivializing almost everything including their jobs. These blends will rather prefer to socialize with people than work, and they tend to take life too casually. However, they've got some natural strengths that enables them to succeed especially in the entertainment and humanitarian sectors, and any career field that is people-oriented where they must always work with people, or attending to different people. Unless they discover their natural strengths early enough, to enable them engage in some private art and craft production works, they will find it difficult working alone or privately without the company of people. Even though they may share some similar qualities with their Sanmel counterparts, and be able to do well in some relevant jobs and careers, but their natural capabilities is no where near those of Sanmel blends, and their light-heartedness will rarely allow them to be as efficient and productive as their Sanmel blend counterparts. Therefore, let us consider some of best jobs or work a Sanphleg personality will be good at, starting off with the entertainment sector.

Best Entertainment Jobs For Sanphleg Personalities:

Sanphlegs are usually very quick to display their skills in the entertainment industry. They are lighthearted entertainers who knows how to impress with their performance, or create something that everyone will admire and compliment them for their skills.

. Comedy/Comic acting,

. Animation,

. Animation director,

. Animal trainer,

. Makeup Artist,

. Costumier,

. Choreography,

. Booking agent,

. Fashion designer,

. Performing artists/musicians.

. Master of Ceremony, MC,

. Illustrator.

The innate creativity of the predominant sanguine combined with the craftiness of the secondary phlegmatic blend plus the congenial and people-oriented qualities of both temperaments makes these personalities light-hearted entertainers who do not find it difficult to succeed in these areas of the entertainment industry.

Best Humanitarian Jobs And Careers For Sanphleg Personalities:

Next to Sanmels are their Sanphleg counterparts when it comes to humanitarian roles that has direct positive impact on the lives of the displaced or downtrodden. The natural enthusiasm and compassionate heart of the sanguine towards others combined with the efficient- organized, calm and collected, and meticulous-patience of the phlegmatic enables a Sanphleg personality to be successful in these jobs. Some of these humanitarian jobs and careers are:

. Pediatric & Child care,

. Elderly care,

. Assistant/helping Nurse,

. Public health officer,

. Social worker,

. Social welfare and rehabilitation,

. Community health worker.

. Reunification officer,

. Public affairs specialist,

. Communications officer,

. Peace officer.

.Best Art Jobs for Sanphleg Personalities:

Apart from the Sanmel and Melsan personalities who comes close, no other blend is more gifted in the production of art works and crafts more than a Sanphleg personality. For the natural creativity of the sanguine combined with the mechanical aptitude and efficiency of the phlegmatic makes a these personality blends standout in physical art and craft making. Some examples of art jobs they are very good at are;

. Painting,

. Drawing,

. Digital artist,

. Performance art,

. Action painting,

. Minimalism,

. Printmaking,

. Dancing,

. Calligraphy,

. Art teaching,

. Creative art director,

. Decorative art,

. Graphic designer,

. Curator.

. All creative craft works.

Best courses for Sanphlegs to study in college:

Sanphleg students needs to discover their innate strengths and qualities with respect to their vocation, in order to choose the best course to study in college that ranks even with their temperament blend strengths and avoid struggling so much in school with little success to show for it. You may have to consider some of the below career fields of study as a

Sanphleg blend. Your natural creativity, people-oriented qualities, and passion for any job that is people-centered will enable you to be efficient in these career fields.

. Linguistics/foreign languages,

. Theatre Art,

. Mass communication,

. Communication studies,

. Film and media arts,

. International relations,

. Fine and applied arts,

. Graphic design,

. Sociology,

. Peace studies and conflict resolution,

. Creative and visual art,

. Marketing,

. Cultural studies,

. Education,

. Social works.

Other Best Jobs and Careers in the public sector for Sanphleg Personalities:

You may have to work in the public sector where you are always required to interact and interface with people, or your job will have to bring you close to the public every time. As a Sanphleg, you are naturally gifted with the qualities to thrive in any public sector job, and get people to easily become attracted to you. Some of these jobs also matched your temperament strengths, and you will find them very interesting.

. Sales and marketing,

. Lower grades classroom teacher,

. Receptionist,

. Customer service,

. Radio/TV presenters,

. Diplomatic Service officer,

. Local Government Officer,

. Public Relations Officer,

Sanphleg personalities usually finds satisfaction and fulfilment in any job or career that makes them build a lasting, solid and cordial interpersonal relationship with people. And also when they are able to make others happy, bring succor and help to the helpless, and have a team of friends, acquaintances, and loyalists who often panders to them because of their congenial and people-oriented qualities.

CHAPTER EIGHT

BEST TECH AND DIGITAL JOBS FOR SANGUINE PERSONALITY BLENDS.

Technological advancements has more job and career and also made tech

"In a technologically dynamic world, our temperament also influences how technologically savvy and dynamic we will be".

innovations and undoubtedly created options in the tech sector, careers more lucrative and highly rewarding in the twenty-first century. Therefore, it will be ill-advised to focus only on the orthodox jobs and careers, and concentrate all your efforts on landing only the traditional jobs with very little to no consideration for the tech and digital sector. The danger of not considering careers in the tech sector, or making effort to improve your tech savviness and landing a job in that sector is that, as technology keeps advancing more and more orthodox or traditional jobs will be automated out of existence, and so many people will be out of job. It's basically for this reason that you have to be passionate about the tech sector, and also be intentional about acquiring a tech skill that will enable you to get a tech or digital job and maybe consider a career in these fields.

In this chapter, while we consider and discuss some traditional jobs that sanguine personalities and blends are best suited for because of their natural strengths and capabilities. It is also very pertinent we give consideration to some jobs and careers in the tech and digital sector that ranks even with the innate strengths and capabilities of the sanguine personality, wherein he will be very successful. Succeeding in the tech sector requires possessing some natural technical capability, intelligence, creative thinking ability, critical and analytical reasoning, organization, and mathematical competence. Even though predominant sanguines lacks some of these basic natural capabilities to effortlessly excel in some high-tech careers, but their natural creativity, sophistication, plus technical ability of their secondary choleric side, and some innate qualities possessed by their melancholy and phlegmatic side will definitely enable them to do very well in certain digital and tech jobs. Let us look at some of the major careers or jobs in the tech industry that sanguine blends are best suited for.

3-D Printing:

The 3-dimensional printing field of the tech sector is an evolving one, and the technology required to effectively 3-D printing jobs is evolving. Any blend of the sanguine personality can succeed as a 3-D printer because of the creative and freehand drawing skills of the predominant sanguine. But I sincerely believe a Sanmel will be head and shoulder above the pack in this field because of the added advantage of the innate perfectionist, thorough, and detailed qualities of the secondary melancholy temperament. While a Sanchol will certainly take advantage of the technical capability and proactivity of the choleric to excel in the field.

Digital video editing:

The ability to manipulate digital video data to create a new video, plus adeptness in the use of video editing Softwares to assemble video clips, add audio tracks, and apply special affects certainly requires the sophistication and technical ability of the Sanchol personality, or the creative thinking ability of the Sanmel plus the analytical and critical thinking qualities of the melancholy to create high quality videos, and be effortlessly successful in the digital video editing career.

Digital Copywriting:

Digital copywriting is an aspect of digital marketing that deals with the creation of advertisement and sales copies about a particular product or service that is capable of convincing the reader to bring out their money and pay for it. These copies are usually created on various digital platforms especially on blogs and websites. The natural creativity of the sanguine combined with the intelligence and critical thinking ability of the melancholy which enables him to read into the minds people to decipher what will attract and interest them, will definitely suffice to enable a Sanmel personality overwhelmingly succeed as a digital copywriter.

Technical writing:

The natural sophistication and technical ability of a typical Sanchol personality or their opposite Cholsan counterpart obviously predisposes him to be the first person to know about the latest technological products and trends. Consequently, writing about these new or latest technical products, Softwares, and appliances and educating people on how to use them is basically what is referred to as technical writing. Asides the choleric blends, a Sanchol personality blend is more naturally equipped to thrive in this job or career.

Digital graphic design:

Almost all three of the sanguine personality blends will do well in this job or career. For the ability to make use of some digital tools to draw or create images sure requires the creativity, knowledge of these tools and how to use them, and freehand drawing skills of the sanguine to create very fine digital images for blogs, website, and any online platform.

Website design:

Web design is basically the process of making websites more user-friendly, having a good or quality interface with web visitors. Website designers are obviously in high demand because of high rate of poorly designed websites with very poor user experience. Apart from the Melsan personality who comes close, no other blend is more naturally gifted with the creative, analytical, innovative, and solution-driven skills of the Sanmel to be able to design a very quality, user-friendly website.

Digital creator:

A digital creator creates contents across all various digital platforms to either market and sell products or information. These contents are usually inform of pictures, videos, and text. Apart from the melancholy personality blends who thrives in this career, sanguine personality blends especially Sanmel blends also do very well as digital creators because of the natural creativity, expression, and communication ability of the sanguine in all the blends, and also the creative and analytical writing ability of the melancholy.

Social media influencer:

The charismatic, assertive, outspokenness, and high sophistication of the Sanchol personality makes him have a lot of followers and those or those who usually panders towards his sophisticated lifestyle on various social media platforms. Consequently, it is not uncommon for his followers to follow almost everything he recommends and give approval to since they already believe in his personality. Apart from a Cholsan or any of the choleric temperament blend who can also succeed as a social media influencer, a typical Sanchol personality is a blend of the sanguine that has the capability to thrive in this job or career.

Web development:

Web development is the process of building and developing a website to function seamlessly in all devices, such as mobile, tablet, and desktop. It is also aimed at optimizing the web speed, and its search engine friendliness through creating contents that will make it visible to major search engines and rank high in search results. The natural creative, technical, and communicative skills of a Sanchol, and the creative and analytical writing ability, plus problem solving, and innovative skills of Sanmel will undoubtedly enable either a Sanchol or Sanmel to effortlessly succeed in web development job and career.

Technical support representative:

The ability to help clients and customers find solutions to their problems, especially when things go wrong with the products or service they've purchased sure requires patience and the passion to help people feel better without being rude or hard towards them. Who but a typical Sanphleg personality has got the patience, light-heartedness, congeniality, and passion to help a visibly unhappy and aggressive client or customer to get the support they need. As a technical support representative, you may not be physically helping clients and customers to resolve their problems, as majority of your job will be online or through some tech support systems. Your job will usually be about answering customer's and client's calls and responding to their questions, sending and responding to emails, and making use of software and tools that will enable you to serve your clients and customers better.

IT Support:

Apart from the choleric blend personalities who comes close because of the technical capability of the choleric, combined with the natural organizational skill of the phlegmatic, and problem solving, creative and analytical thinking ability of melancholy. Sanguine blends are also very good IT support personnel who helps to ensure that all IT systems of an organization are functioning properly without any hitch because of their communicative skills and adeptness in tech. The strong skill required to be an IT support agent is your knowledge of the ICT.

Conclusively, by nature, predominant sanguine personalities and their choleric counterparts are technically savvy people, hence their seamless and effortless sophistication in tech. Consequently, any job or career in the digital and tech sector requiring some natural soft skills such as; communication, creative, analytical, and critical thinking skills, plus problem solving and organizational skills will doubtlessly be suitable for sanguine personality blends.

CHAPTER NINE

CAREER ADVANCEMENT STRATEGIES FOR SANGUINE PERSONALITIES.

> "Natural advancement is involuntary, career advancement thrives on intentionality"

Perhaps you've taken the discovering the best personality. And you've developed yourself in has obviously landed important question is, right steps towards career path for your also to an extent that career path which you a good job. The next what next? This question is apt because nothing in life is static, more so in this vast, technologically dynamic space together with the very competitive society we find ourselves. No one can afford to be static in their career, else you would be left behind and could become irrelevant and ill-fated in your chosen career. In this chapter, we want to consider some smart career management strategies you must adopt for your career advancement in order to steadily improve yourself in your field and become so useful in it, as well as the go-to person in that career field.

First off, what's career management? Career management has got basically to do with how you personally control and manage your career development process. There are some basic strategies you've got to adopt in order to effectively manage how you will advance further in your career particularly as a predominant sanguine personality in this context. Having said that and without taking much time, let's begin to consider some of these basic career management strategies that will enable you better manage your career development efforts and subsequently advance in your career path.

Career Management Strategies For Career Advancement:

Career advancement in the twenty-first century requires being deliberate about adopting some management strategies that will enable you to advance in your career until you hit the highest height in it. Let us consider some of these strategies and how they can help you advance in your career as a sanguine.

1. Self-educate:

Self-education is one of the key smart career management strategies you must adopt in order to get ahead of your competitors. It's basically the process of deliberately educating yourself and acquiring more relevant skills and knowledge that will get you on the path of emerging as the best in your field. Self-education can be done through online research on search engines. Downloading, purchasing and reading books, eBooks and journals that are relevant to your chosen career field with the primary intention of gaining more professional knowledge and be ahead of your colleagues. Every temperament can actually self- educate whether they do it remotely from their homes or going for regular lectures and tutorials outside their home. The basic thing is to be deliberate about it, and be consistent with it.

In order to effectively educate yourself and have it reflect in your career endeavors, you must jot down some important and relevant points. Then go back to reading them, and perhaps create a catalog for all extraneous takeaways that you will often refer back to anytime you want to update yourself. In this digital and information age, self-education is one of the basic ways if not the best way so many people are using to learn new things and updating themselves in their field through the internet. It's a very effective and efficient strategy you can adopt to manage your career and be ahead of the pack.

2. Personal Development:

Your career advancement efforts will be completely in jeopardy if you do not personally develop and improve yourself. Personal development is the process of building your personality in how you write, communicate, think, relate with people, appear and comport yourself in public spaces. People will often address you first of all, according to your appearance before they will attempt to know who you are and what you do. You could have worked so hard to build a very good and solid career for yourself but without improving your lifestyle, you may not go far in getting to the summit of your career. You don't want to ruin your career or let your hard work become an effort in futility because of some little lows in your lifestyle. Career development and advancement goes beyond just improving and advancing in your career. It encompasses all facets of your existence as a person. While you are making effort to build your career you need to also consider improving your lifestyle and attitude. It's a very key smart strategy for effective career management and advancement.

3. Invest In Your Career:

There's no way you can build yourself or your career without investing your money, effort, time, and resources. Career management requires some financial investments for you to be able to get to the zenith of your career. Success is about being deliberate about what you want, and knowing what you've got to do to achieve your goals. No one can be successful in anything without first having the desire and passion to succeed. Personal career management is the financial commitments you've got to make to advance in your career and be ahead of others. You don't need to wait for your organization to do that for you, even though some companies and big organizations could sometime send their staffs for some professional training and courses. But if you want to be exceptional in your job, and make your employers see you as a key assert, then you have to be financially responsible for your personal career development. Career management is a journey you must financially commit yourself to, if you really want to make yourself relevant and indispensable to your organization.

Choleric personalities, and maybe melancholies to some extent quite understands the importance of personally investing in their career. No wonder cholerics are always ahead of others in any organization because they are very ambitious people, who often likes to be ahead in everything. They do not need to wait for management to invest in them by sending them on courses before they'll go for training. They simply go before others, then come back to take challenging tasks, which consequently facilitates their promotion. Investing in your career is one of the smart career management strategy you must adopt to advance in your career. As a sanguine, you need to be more deliberate about this, delay instant gratification and overindulgence and invest in developing yourself so you can advance in your career.

4. Improve Your Interpersonal Skills:

Interpersonal skills is one of the basic soft skill many organizations require from job seekers. This skill is essential to build interpersonal relationships with other staffs or personnel sin order to achieve the organization's goals and objective. Without a good interpersonal skills, interpersonal working relationship with others will be difficult, and this will negatively impact on your career development pursuit. Thus, improving your interpersonal skills is another important career management strategy you must adopt in order to holistically build your career and achieve career success. Sanguines and Phlegmatics may not have much problem relating very well with others. But sanguines must show more seriousness, discipline and also diligence to work, while phlegmatics must learn to make sacrifices and courageous enough to take on new challenges.

As for cholerics and melancholies, cholerics have got the least developed interpersonal skills, they must sure work on that if they want to achieve career success. Melancholies have got all the qualities they require to excel in their career, including the basic interpersonal skill. But they certainly need to work on their moodiness, pessimistic and perfectionist traits, which often tends to become a clog in their wheel of career advancement.

5. Build Connections:

Human beings are made to connect with one another. No one is an island, or can exist in isolation. It's for this reason that you must endeavor to build connection and connect with others who may or may not be directly linked with the same career field as you. As you can see, the world has now become a global village since you no longer necessarily need to physically be with people or see them before conversation could take place. Networking has become easier since the advent of internet, and the social media. A lot of persons are now leveraging on the social networking sites such as; Facebook, Twitter, LinkedIn, Instagram etc. to build links and stay connected with their friends, family or colleagues. For you as a careerist, who wants to advance in your career, the best social media platform you ought not to neglect is LinkedIn.

LinkedIn is where career enthusiast and professionals like you are found. They use it to build relationship and connect with other professionals in their field. Through it, you can know what people in your industry are doing, and keep yourself up to date about trending and emerging trends in your career. Building connections around your industry is another smart career management strategy you must adopt in order to advance in your career and reach the summit of it.

6. See And Take Advantage Of Opportunities:

One of the smart career management strategy you must intentionally fuse into your career development plans is, to see and take advantage of every opportunity you've got to advance your career before others. Different opportunities are often presented to us perhaps sometimes unknowingly, for we to leverage on, and take our career to the next level. But how fast we are able to identify these various opportunities and take advantage of them, is what gets us ahead of others, and high-up there easily. Passing over opportunities repeatedly is rarely a smart attitude or lifestyle for anyone that's desirous of attaining career success. It will not only make you regret not taking action when you're supposed to, but will also leave you unfulfilled and unaccomplished as an individual. Every opportunity you've got to broaden or deepen your career is definitely not to be neglected or toiled with, if you want to be very impactful in your career.

7. Manage Your Temperament Weaknesses:

Every temperament has got different weaknesses and strengths. It is very pertinent that while you are utilizing your temperament strengths to build your career, you've got to also identify the inherent weaknesses associated with your basic temperament and know how to manage them. The sanguine's major weakness that often negatively affects his career advancement, is his complacency, indiscipline, lack of commitment and steadfastness. Sanguines needs to work on themselves in these areas. For cholerics, they've got everything it takes to succeed and get to the zenith of their career. But they must manage some of their temperament weaknesses of poor interpersonal relationship, inconsiderateness, high-handedness and aggression.

Predominant sanguine personalities must learn how to manage their individual temperament weaknesses that affects their lifestyles through interactions, which consequently will have a considerable amount of influence of the strengths of other temperaments on them. Since a temperament like melancholy possess strengths and qualities that are markedly opposite of the weaknesses of a sanguine, it will not take him a long time to be influenced by these strengths if he consistently relate with the melancholy, and vice versa. In conclusion, everyone has got what it takes to succeed in any career they choose as long it conforms with their natural temperament. But they must do well to identify their individual weaknesses and make efforts towards ameliorating them in order to clear any impediments on the way to advancing their careers.

6 BASIC THINGS TO CONSIDER BEFORE CONTEMPLATING A CAREER CHANGE.

It is absolutely possible ourselves in careers or our personality and as a to cope with its descriptions, plus we and unproductive in it.

that we may find jobs that does not define result, we often struggle specifications and become so mechanical Such careers may also be time and energy draining and consuming since the motivation to effortlessly and efficiently take on it is obviously lacking. I've discovered that the worst careers are those that we struggle to become productive in, and they thus needlessly take all our time and do not give us the leverage to explore other options. We struggle to meet deadlines, keep track of innovations, and we become completely dissatisfied with such careers.

These are simply not the "best careers that describes our personality. It could be for this reason that you may want to consider a career change. However, different persons have got different reasons why they want to change their career and explore other options and opportunities. But for whatever reason that you may want to contemplate changing your career, do not forget to factor in these six things. Because they will not only help you to be aware of the setbacks in that particular career, but will also help you to excel in it, and will also undoubtedly make you become self-reliant and independent even after you retire and become a private citizen. Therefore, let's go straight off to considering these six things you've got to factor in before contemplating a career change.

1. Temperament Compatibility:

After marriage, our career is the next thing we have to be very choosey and circumspect about before making that lifelong decision. Therefore, anyone who is passionate about efficiency and productiveness in their chosen career, and want to have a sense of fulfilment and satisfaction, one major thing you should consider is how such career is in conformity or compatible with the basic temperament you're born with. Every temperament has got different personality traits that makes everyone unique in their own right. We may all be able to succeed in different fields of endeavor through hard work and discipline. But not all of us can effortlessly and creatively succeed in the same things when it becomes so tough and challenging. It's for this reason that some persons will stumble and fall along the way, and will definitely not reach the zenith of their chosen career. However, the same person that could not navigate through, and get to highest level in that particular endeavor is able to do so and achieve success in another.

This obviously gives credence to the fact that we're distinct human beings in nature, differently talented and gifted in specific areas of endeavors in life. Therefore, if you're dissatisfied in your present career and perhaps, contemplating a career change. The first thing you would want to consider is, how your new career is compatible with your temperament strengths and qualities. To what extent is your personality traits agreeable with your intended or proposed career path. This is absolutely invaluable to avoid becoming a square peg in a round hole and perhaps become worst off, in your new career path.

2. Prospects In The Career:

Career prospects is another important factor to consider when considering a change in career. Every career has got various prospects and opportunities that needs to be explored and taken advantage of. And these available opportunities are the incentives and motivating factors that will compel you to aspire for greater heights in the career, and become exceptional. If a particular career does not have good enough available opportunities and prospects, then there's no point trying to expend your energy and resources on improving yourself in it. Therefore, to avoid making a mistake in choosing or changing your career, you need to consider the prospects and opportunities available in such career. So you don't find yourself in a dungeon where you could have something so invaluable to offer that no one needs.

3. Competitiveness:

In this digital and information age, there is obviously high level of competitions in different careers. Highly competitive careers often limits your chances of being found or noticed by different organizations or prospective clients and customers. It's for this reason that you will need to consider to what extent is your intended career competitive. Is it highly-competitive, low or even non-competitive? Careers that have low or non-competitiveness but have high prospects are easily the most rewarding, and in high demand. Competitiveness is what you will need to consider when you are contemplating a change in your career. If it's a highly competitive one, how are you going to navigate through, and become the go-to-person in that career? What strategies do you have to outshine and outsmart those who are already there before you? These are some of the salient questions you need to answer before considering a career change.

4. Career Advancement:

Any career that will not give you the leverage to improve yourself and advance in it, is not worth considering. A good and decent career is expected to give you the ample time and opportunity to advance yourself in it and reach the highest level in your organization. If you find it hard to advance in a particular career, and grow from one level to another while maintaining a balance between it and your private life, then you've got to reconsider remaining in such career. However, how you will advance in your new and intended career is another important factor you should put into consideration when contemplating a career change. Because, this will help you to make the right career choice, plus deepen yourself in it, and also reach the highest career cadre in your organization or as a private person. I believe the seven strategies listed in chapter nine will definitely help you to answer this question.

5. Time Leverage:

Twenty-four hours a day may not suffice for anyone aspiring to beat the deadline in pursuing a particular goal, either organizational or personal goal and objectives. Sometimes, we need more time to achieve more or do other things, but more often than not, time is not really enough because it's of essence, and the only thing that cannot be recovered when lost. If you're in any career or job that makes you work more than the normal eight hours a day, then you will obviously need more time to do other things, and achieve personal success. I've discovered that the worst, and sometimes less rewarding careers are those that often drains our energy and also consumes all our time, that we do not have time for ourselves or for other things. If you're in a career that makes you work longer time than necessary and tiresomely also, rather than effortlessly to achieve a particular goal, and does not also give you the time leverage to perhaps embark on other profitable ventures, then you shouldn't be in that career and you need to start considering a career change. Any career that will allow you the time to explore other options and probably have a side business or run any other profitable venture is what you should consider in these day and age.

6. Sustainability And Self-sufficiency:

A lot of persons becomes very useless to themselves and their families after years of active service and retirement. This is obviously because; firstly, they did not choose a career that they can turn to their private business. And secondly, probably they never see the business opportunities in that career. Some persons retired and decides to turn their career or jobs they've put in many years of service into their personal or private business ventures. This enables them to remain relevant in society while still making some cool money for themselves. Careers that have sustainability, and one that will make you become self-sufficient after you retire from active years of service are those you should consider when contemplating a change in career. This is necessary to enable you scale through and overcome the boredom and inactiveness, plus the financial bankruptcy that comes with retirement. Therefore, before you go ahead to decide on any career path or contemplate changing career, you ought to ask yourself, how sustainable is that career. And will it make me to be self-sufficient by engaging in a profitable venture that is relevant to that career when I retire from service?

Conclusively, in this age and time where unemployment rate is high, it is best to insist on careers that ranks even with our temperament strengths and capabilities, those that will enable us to remain active, productive, and self-sufficient even after we are retired. For the experience garnered in years of active practice of that career or profession, or that matched our temperament strengths and qualities will doubtlessly enable us to quickly turn them into profitable ventures, remain productive, and self-sufficient for very long time.

BEST LUCRATIVE BUSINESSES FOR PREDOMINANT SANGUINES.

In these days of high scarcity of jobs. It's begin to look beyond for some big

"To become an employer you must kill an employee mentality".

unemployment, and important that we must working for someone or organizations, to creating job for ourselves and become self-reliant or Self-employed. But it's quite unfortunate that in this age and time, most young school leavers and graduates still think that the main reason for acquiring a formal education is so they will be able to get some white- collar jobs which are very scarce and maybe non-existent. The main reason for acquiring formal education isn't just about getting a white-collar job or pursuing a formal career in companies and very big organizations. But it's rather about exposing some hidden potentials in you that you can unleash to become very exceptional in what you do, open up a wide variety of opportunities to you, that you could take advantage of in becoming your own boss.

It's basically for this reason that in this chapter, we want to consider some profitable and lucrative business opportunities that matched the predominant sanguine personality's temperament strengths that if deliberately considered will enable him become self-employed, self-reliant, and his own boss. Therefore, in this chapter, we'll be considering some major business ventures that best describes the sanguine's personality, that he could venture into, and become self-reliant. There are numerous benefits of being self-employed. Firstly, you will be your own boss. Secondly, you will be financially independent, and lastly you will also have the opportunity of creating jobs for others. So many persons have become entrepreneurs and CEO's through self-employment.

They never had to wait for any white collar job which are non-existent by the way. But they were deliberate and determined about being self-reliant, they started very small, and worked very hard until their business became a brand. Therefore, if you want to become self-reliant, you must be deliberate about creating job for yourself, and start thinking like an entrepreneur. The following businesses listed in this chapter are those that ranks even with the sanguine's temperament strengths, they are very profitable, and easy to setup and manage, if taken advantage of. They can easily be run and managed by a sanguine because they measure up to his natural capabilities. Let's quickly look at them one after the other. But Remember, these businesses were chosen in consideration of who a sanguine is, and some of the natural strengths and talents that will enable him to effortlessly succeed in them. However turning your career into a business, or managing a business is another different thing entirely that no doubt requires experience and competence. You may not exactly have to go to Harvard business school, but you sure need to acquire some business skills and competence to be able to turn you career into business and also manage it efficiently.

Promotion And Marketing Business:

Based on the fact that a sanguine is a very charismatic and people-oriented personality. Therefore, going into a self-reliant career in marketing and sales is very advisable and profitable as well. Registering a business name with the objective of promoting and marketing other people's businesses, and also helping them to generate six figure leads is sales, is no doubt a very profitable business venture. Marketing/promotion and sales are one career you can turn into a very profitable business and become your own boss, rather than wait to be hired or employed by manufacturing and service business organizations. The business prospects in this career is that a lot of manufacturing and service businesses are looking to make their products and services go viral, and get to the least person on the street, and even to the remotest part of a region. Consequently, these organizations are willing to outsource their marketing and promotion plans to other agencies for effective marketing, in order to achieve high sales and turnover.

Therefore, as a predominant sanguine personality, you've got the natural charisma, people-oriented qualities and word-of-mouth to help businesses and organizations achieve their goals and objectives of efficient marketing and sales. Therefore, establishing a promotion and marketing agency for the sole aim of helping businesses and organizations drives sales or become a brand is no doubt the best decision you have to make. It's hitherto one of the best business or self-reliant career you can turn into a profitable business venture.

Public Relations And Marketing Agency:

In similar way to helping businesses to market and promote their goods and services through your promotion and marketing agency. Public relation and marketing is a way of laundering people's image, or maybe the image of a particular organization that has lost credibility, and bring back people's confidence to it. PR marketing is the process of selling or marketing a particular person or organization to the public, in order to get the support, and have the confidence of the public reposed in the person or that organization. As a typical sanguine, you've got the oratory, word-of-mouth and also the communicative ability to woo anyone to believe in what you're trying to sell to them. These strengths are basic in helping you to excel in this business venture. You may decide to start a Public relations and marketing agency by registering a business name with the main objective of standing in the gap for a person especially a politician, group of persons or an organization. You could be hired by individuals and political parties for image laundering, especially during electioneering campaign periods, to woo people to their side. You can also be hired by organizations for positive publicity or to bring back their lost credibility.

Travel And Tour Agency:

As a sanguine, you love adventures. Travelling and going on tours, making new friends are part of your lifestyle. You're the first to become versatile and conversant about a place before any other person. Therefore, starting a travel and tour agency, where you help to book flights, organize travels or tours to different countries, states or regions for people, and also educate them about the place and lifestyle of the people is no doubt one of the profitable business venture that will make you self-reliant and be your own boss. This business has got great prospects, because a lot of people loves visiting different places and traveling to many different countries around the world. Some of them have never been to this places before, hence they need more guidelines and information about those places before going there. They sometimes also do need someone to plan and arrange for their travelling, and also advice them appropriately about those countries.

As a sanguine, who is usually more vast and may have got more experiences about these places because of your adventurous and traveling lifestyle. No other person is better qualified to guide intending visitors to those places more than you. Travels and tours agency are in more demands now than ever before, because a lot of persons are increasingly visiting and going to unfamiliar countries for which they will need some traveling tips and guidance.

Hospitality And Recreation:

Since you're a people-oriented person who loves to make everyone feel very relaxed and comfortable, with your charisma and ebullience. Going into a hospitality and recreation business as a sanguine will be a very good one for you. You don't need to have so much money to go into this business, all you need is a little space or small piece of land and make it look very cozy and attractive. People often loves to chill and relax in a very serene and beautiful area after the days work and activities. Thus, if you've got a small piece of land, or a little space preferably in a not very much noisy environment. You could develop and make it more beautiful, and equipped with some recreational facilities, and people especially visitors and guests from other places will pay you to relax their and make use of those facilities. A lot of persons have come to own very big hospitality businesses like five star hotels and big recreation centers through starting a small event and relaxation center. And since you're a sanguine who knows how to attract people's attention, you will not struggle to make it in this business.

Showbiz And Entertainment:

This list will not be complete without talking about entertainment and showbiz. As a sanguine, you've got passion for entertainment, either you are the entertainer or you're being entertained. You love to make people feel happy and comfortable. If this is your passion, then starting a showbiz, entertainment and also event center business is no doubt one of the most profitable business for your personality. You could start your own music and video production studio, video game center, comedy club, fun events and entertainment centers, where people usually come to get entertained, thus helping them ease their stress or boredom. People loves to be entertained, and this is basically the major prospects in this career. When you've got such a business outfit, you could also enroll other young and upcoming entertainers into your business organization, and mentor them while charging them a little fee.

Entertainment and showbiz are very big business in the world right now. Because people loves to have fun and enjoy themselves, perhaps because of some very unfavorable situations and circumstances a lot of persons are going through, hence the need to chill out and relax somewhere, and forget about those unfortunate moments.

Creative Art Works Business:

As a predominant sanguine personality, you are naturally a very creative person who easily expresses emotions, feelings, and have the ability to visualize something into reality. Therefore, since art is an unstructured form of work that usually expresses emotions, feelings, and visions, it's not uncommon for you to effortlessly and exceptionally be very successful in the production of various art works that people can easily relate to. Some of the creative art works you can engage in, and turn into a profitable venture are; painting, sculpture, calligraphy, printmaking, photography, drawing, fine arts, and any creative art works that appeals to the feelings and sensibility of people. There is very high prospect in the creative art works business because so many art lovers all over the world appreciate these art products, and also spends a lot of money to acquire them for beautification, decoration, or reflection purposes.

In conclusion, as a predominant sanguine, you are very talented, and possess unique creative skills that are rare in other temperaments. However, this natural creativity and talents are more often than not overshadowed by your lack of self-discipline, focus, steadfastness, and overindulgence. But if you can be more deliberate about deploying your natural talent and creativity into profitable ventures, you will certainly be on the right path to becoming your own boss.

CHAPTER TWELVE

MAJOR WEAKNESS OF THE SANGUINE TEMPERAMENT AND HOW TO OVERCOME IT.

Lack of self-discipline is major, if not number one <u>sanguine personality</u>. If bit closely with a will definitely not take that lack of self- unarguably one of the <u>weakness of the</u> you interact and relate a predominant sanguine, it you too long to observe discipline is one of his

> "Along with our natural temperament strengths also comes corresponding weaknesses".

main natural oddity in life. Even from a distance, his exuberant and effervescent lifestyle is rarely concealed, they are so glaring that you can immediately decipher how undisciplined he is. His overindulgent and enjoying lifestyle are the major culprits of his lack of self-discipline and self-control. The sanguine is overly an enjoying person who usually enjoys freedom a lot, and is so much addicted to fun and pleasure. Nothing hurts him more than denying him the freedom to live his flamboyant and exuberant lifestyle . He is as free as air. No wonder he is rightly described as the air personality in the temperament theory of Hippocrates. The will to subject himself to either self-made or general rules, or deny himself some few moments of funfair and pleasure is almost lacking.

Lack of self-discipline and self-control is no doubt the main undoing of most sanguines in life. It's more often than not responsible for his inability to meet his set goals, earn the trust and respect of others and achieve personal success either in his personal endeavors as an individual or his job and career. He may decide to prepare or schedule his personal reading timetable as a student, but fun and pleasurable times and hanging out with friends and admirers will rarely allow him to religiously follow through to his reading timetable. He could also make a rule in his home, that no one stays late outside beyond 8p.m, but trust that he will be the first culprit to break his own rules. His inadvertent consistency in breaking his own rules, often makes his wife and kids and everyone who is close to him to become accustomed to his undisciplined lifestyle, and perhaps begin to take his rules and decisions for granted, and as an unserious person.

In his personal endeavors, apart from the typical phlegmatic who comes close there is rarely any other temperament that blusters or brags about starting so many things but seldom completes or achieves any like a sanguine. Unlike his typical phlegmatic counterpart, who may have dreams or the desire to start a project, but lacks the courage to start it unless he's being pushed. But the sanguine may start different things at the same time or take initial steps to achieving his dreams and personal goals but rarely will he be steadfast and commit himself to achieving any of those. For he usually gets bored easily doing a particular thing consistently, especially if he does not see immediate results and successes. Sometimes, fun and pleasure, and immediate gratification can also make him to mindlessly abandon the project he had started, regardless of the amount of time, resources, and effort he had put into it. In addition to this, like his phlegmatic counterpart, typical sanguine easily surrenders to challenges or hard times. Abandoning his goals, dreams or visions immediately he is confronted by any challenge or difficult situations along the way is not uncommon for him. It is for these reasons that personal achievements and successes usually eludes the predominant sanguine personality.

When it comes to his job or career, unless the job affords him the leverage to meet or interact with different persons where he will be able to display his flamboyance talkativeness, and exuberance, no other temperament often changes job more than the predominant sanguine person. It is rare to see a typical sanguine put in almost a decade of his life working for a particular company or organization and remain in job role and responsibility that do not give him something new and interesting to relish for all his efforts. He usually gets bored with routines that doesn't allow him the freedom and opportunity to freely express himself as much as he would like to. Jobs that requires routines, so much seriousness, carefulness, attention-to-details, critical and analytical thinking skills and self-discipline easily bores him. He is very adventurous, and always enjoys some new and exciting opportunities. Therefore, changing jobs so frequently is not an uncommon thing for him. Among all of the weaknesses and idiosyncrasies of a typical sanguine, lack of self-discipline seems to be the bane of his success in life. Since discipline is one of the main ingredients of success, and also a major attributes of successful people. It's mainly for this reason that we want to look at some of the ways a typical sanguine can overcome lack of self-discipline and become a more resolute and organized person. Therefore, let us look at these five ways a predominant sanguine personality can overcome or at least manage this natural weakness associated with his temperament.

1. Through Influence:

I have often make it clear that **influence** is one of the ways by which we can overcome or at least, manage most of the weaknesses that are inherent in the temperaments we are born with. As a predominant sanguine, you've no doubt got some strengths which could be deficient or lacking in the other temperaments, just the same way the other temperaments have also got some qualities and strengths you're also destitute of. But, our inherited temperament strengths also accompanies with it natural corresponding weaknesses, which we rarely pay attention to or do not want to talk about. But if we're honest with ourself, we must establish the fact that the first step to self-improvement is to realize that these weaknesses do exist in us and accept the fact that we need to do away with them. And one way we could do away with them or make their impact become less impactful on us, is through exchange of influence of our temperament strengths and qualities. As humans, we're more often attracted to the strengths and qualities of others, while their weaknesses do irritates us. Thus, it will be much easier for us to be positively influenced by their strengths or qualities rather than their natural oddities and weaknesses.

Therefore, as a predominant sanguine who lacks self-discipline and determination, by interacting and relating more closely with some temperaments that epitomizes these strengths and qualities you will gradually and unconsciously become influenced by these strengths and qualities subsequently. The temperaments that has got the natural strengths of self-discipline, self-control and determination are mainly melancholy and choleric temperaments. Although, these two temperaments also possess some natural weaknesses which could be strengthened or improved by your own natural strengths as a typical sanguine. But when it comes to overcoming, or at least managing your weaknesses of indiscipline, lack of self-control and determination they are no doubt the best personalities that you ought to relate more closely with, and also need to have a very good number of them as your close friends and companions.

Though, their weaknesses may bore you at first, but for the basic reason that you love and admire and also feels attracted to their strengths and qualities, that should suffice to keep you interested in them if you are honest and intentional about overcoming your weaknesses. You will discover that the more closely you interact and relate with a predominant melancholy personality or someone who has got melancholy-choleric blend, the more their strengths or qualities of self-discipline, self-determination and resoluteness rubs off on you. Consequently, you will gradually see those weaknesses associated with your predominant sanguine temperament being strengthened and improved by the perfectionist melancholy strengths and qualities, while the melancholy person will also benefit from your charisma, optimism and expressiveness. This is basically how the back and forth influence of our temperament strengths do help us ameliorate the negative impacts of our personality weaknesses on us, and also shapes our personality.

2. Learning From The Experience Of Others:

I've come to realize that life's experiences oftentimes seems to be the best teacher. But do you have to wait until you experience the negative side of life before you will learn? Of course, no. So it is basically for this reason that other's experiences should be a lesson to us. To either make us take precautions not to repeat their mistakes, or learn from how they succeeded, and use it to enhance our own pursuit of success. Having some more experienced persons share their life's experiences with you, either their negative or positive experiences, is one of the best ways you can be more deliberate about managing, and knowledgeable about how to overcome or at least manage your temperament weaknesses.

Remember you are not the only sanguine person battling with lack of self-discipline and determination, all predominant sanguine personalities with at least, up to 60 percent sanguine traits also faces these challenge in life. Some may have probably battled with these weaknesses and were able to manage or overcome it, and are still alive to tell their story or share their experiences of how it initially hindered them from making progress in pursuit of their dreams and personal goals, and how they later became successful in life. And others who could not succeed in life because of these natural weaknesses, lived to gripe over it, and blamed them self for the rest of their life.

It's basically for this reason that learning from some of the past experiences of those who had battled with similar challenge or weaknesses of lack of self-discipline and self-determination. Perhaps they have similar sanguine temperament just like yourself, learning from their experience is one of the most effective way of managing, and subsequently overcoming these weaknesses. You may have to attend some motivational seminars to listen and learn from some of these life coaches, or buy and read books that were written by them. One of the best books I'll recommend you order and read to help you conquer indiscipline and be a master of yourself is, going from undisciplined to self-mastery written by Harris Kern.

3. Develop Your Secondary Temperament:

Every human being possesses more than one temperament, some even have more than two but they will usually be in varying degrees or proportions. This is very possible because temperament is an inherited traits which we inherited from our parents and even more from our grandparents as result of their genes and chromosomes that were transferred to us during our conception. For instance, your grandpa and grandma could be, say predominantly sanguine and phlegmatic respectively as a result, traits of sanguine and phlegmatic will for sure be transferred to your immediate parents. And if perhaps your grandparents also possessed some melancholy and choleric traits which they most likely inherited from their own parents, some of these traits will definitely be passed on to your parents also, perhaps in little amount. Therefore, your parents are very much likely to inherit blends of all these temperaments with either sanguine or phlegmatic as their primary or dominant temperament depending on which of their parents they took more genes from during their conception. Now, if your parents are let's say primarily sanguine and phlegmatic respectively, you are no doubt likely to inherit traits of these temperaments from either of them that has got their genes and chromosomes transferred to you in excess. You could also go way back to inheriting more genes and chromosomes from either your grandma or grandpa, which could have some of their melancholic or choleric traits passed on to you. Whether it is your immediate parents or grandparents you've got more of their genes transferred to you, you will no doubt carry traits of their primary temperament, while the others that were transferred to you in lesser amount will certainly be your secondary temperament. It's basically from this concept that we have the temperament blends and combinations.

Having established the concept of <u>blends of temperaments</u> and how it came about, it is therefore necessary for us to know that our secondary temperament is also as very important as our primary. Therefore, we ought to be very conscious of it, and take it seriously the same we are always conscious of our primary temperament in order to benefit from its strengths and qualities. Being conscious of our secondary temperament, developing its strengths, and allowing it to also have some positive influence on our attitude and behavioral pattern like our primary temperament is no doubt one of the ways we can also manage or maybe overcome our weaknesses. You could be a 60 or 70 percent predominantly sanguine, with 40 or 30 percent choleric, phlegmatic or melancholic. That is, you may be either a Sanchol, Sanphleg or Sanmel of 60:40, 70: 30 or even 55:45 blend ratios. All of these secondary temperaments have got considerable amount of self-discipline and control. Thus, they will usually once in a while influence our behavioral patterns, what we do, and how we do things. Consequently, yielding more frequently to their positive influence on us, will gradually develop and establish their inherent strengths, and also help to cover up for, or lessen the negative impacts of our predominant temperament weaknesses on us. Therefore as someone who has sanguine as a predominant temperament, you have to also be aware of, and identify your secondary temperament and its innate strengths and qualities. Then be deliberate about developing it by yielding more often to its influences. This also will help you to manage or possibly overcome weaknesses of lack of self-discipline and control.

4. Have The Right Motivation For Success:

Sometimes not having something that constantly and consistently motivates you to go ahead and pursue your dreams, or strive for success will make you live your life carelessly like someone without a direction in life. It's not until you begin to stand up for something, you will definitely fall for everything that comes your way. Most sanguines usually live their lives without a direction. They rarely have focus or the right motivation for the goals and dreams they want to achieve in life. Hence, living for the present isn't uncommon for them. Therefore, the will to regulate or moderate their overindulgent lifestyle is basically lacking, since they've got nothing to protect, stand up for, or worry themself about. It's mainly for this reason that they could afford to live their lives without any form of self-discipline and restraint. But if you want to overcome or at least manage your weakness of lack of self-discipline as a typical sanguine, you must be deliberate about having the right passion and motivation for your personal success and always work towards the actualization of your dreams.

There's more to life than just living very flamboyantly in merriment, enjoyment. And predominant sanguines needs to realize this if they want to achieve personal success in life, or accomplish very remarkable things. Even God did not plan that man should live all his life in idleness and merriment. No wonder he gave Adam some work to do in the garden even before the fall. And there's certainly no time for fun and enjoyment when you're working. Therefore, as a predominant sanguine, much as you would want to indulge yourself in fun and some pleasurable moments but you must also ensure that you're not doing that at the expense of being productive.

You must be intentional about engaging yourself and spending very considerable amount of your time in some profitable or productive ventures that will add value to not just your life, but also to the lives of others around you. Rather than just being out there with friends and admirers to bluster, giggle and always exhibit your exuberant lifestyles. You may decide for instance, to use your natural charisma, liveliness, congenial and people-oriented qualities plus storytelling ability to market or sell products, organize, and set up a comedy club for shows and entertainments, or maybe get yourself involved in some social service works like rehabilitating people, turning them from very depressed to hopeful and lively human beings. These are some of the areas you can deploy your strengths as a typical sanguine, and become more productive in life. You will gradually become a more self-disciplined and organized sanguine when you consistently engage yourself in more productive and profitable ventures in life.

CONCLUSION.

In the temperament theory of Hippocrates, sanguines are described as air. Like air, they are free, prevalent, and appears to be too common but very important for human coexistence as long as human interpersonal relationship is concerned. The world has immensely benefitted from the enrichment of the sanguine temperament because of the creativity, happy-charisma, humor, and interpersonal skills associated with this temperament type. Almost all of the art works in the world that we admire, which tends to make us reflect on history, relate to, and also depict emotions are created by predominant sanguine, or at least someone who their secondary temperament is sanguine.

These air personalities cannot be caged or confined, else they will explode and quickly erupt like a volcano; for freedom is their basic mantra. Whatever that affects a predominant sanguine's freedom to freely express himself usually affects his emotions which could make him erupt in quick explosive outburst. When it comes to vocation, the sanguine personality is enormously gifted and talented in various aspects. He is naturally a creative person, gifted in helping people, and he has the persuasive ability and happy- charisma to attract friends and endear himself to them. However, his lack of self-discipline, focus, and purposefulness usually makes him unable to discover his worth and how to make use of his admirable qualities and abilities to add value to life, consequently abandoning his core mandate in life. But he usually seem to concentrate more on the easier part of his life, which is finding it convenient to relate to with everyone and always be in a convivial mood with people, while jettisoning his natural creative ability that could make him positively impactful, and a force to reckon with if rightly deployed. Any career that is people-oriented enough where he could express himself and display his flamboyance and exuberance are usually those that seems to attract him. But he must look inwards to discover that much more than his congeniality and people-oriented qualities, he is got some natural creative abilities that can be harnessed and effectively deployed in order to achieve personal success.

108

109

111

112